Classes in Modern Society
Elites and Society
Sociology: A Guide to Problems and Literature

CRITICS OF SOCIETY

RADICAL THOUGHT IN NORTH AMERICA

T. B. BOTTOMORE

CRITICS

OF

PANTHEON BOOKS

A Division of Random House, Inc., New York

SOCIETY

Radical Thought
in North America

FIRST AMERICAN EDITION

© Copyright, 1968, by T. B. Bottomore

All rights reserved under International and Pan American Copyright Conventions. Published in New York by Pantheon Books, a division of Random House, Inc. Originally published in Canada as "Social Criticism in North America" © Copyright, 1966, by Canadian Broadcasting Corporation.

Library of Congress Catalog Card Number: 67-19181

Manufactured in the United States of America by The Haddon Craftsmen, Inc., Scranton, Pa.

PREFACE

This book originated in a series of talks which I gave for the *Ideas* program of the Canadian Broadcasting Corporation between March and May 1966. The talks have been published by the C.B.C. under the title *Social Criticism in North America*. In revising and expanding the text for this edition I have aimed to discuss more fully the views of some major social critics and to present in greater detail the background to their ideas. I have also added a bibliography as a guide to further reading on American radicalism. But I have not attempted to alter fundamentally the character of the work, which I offer as a tentative essay in the interpretation of radical social thought. In particular, I have not ventured upon an account of social and political movements, except briefly in discussing the new radicalism of the 1960s. This would require a different and much longer book. My chief concern has been with the connections between intellectual dissent and theories of society; a subject unduly neglected by historians of social thought, and nowhere more so than in the United States. The heritage of American radical thought—with all its achievements, limitations and defeats—should be of particular interest at the present time when radicalism is on the upsurge again but is still groping for an adequate form of intellectual expression.

CONTENTS

CRITICS OF SOCIETY

RADICAL THOUGHT IN NORTH AMERICA

CHAPTER 1

THE

GROWTH

OF

CRITICISM

Social criticism, in one form or another, has had a place in most human societies. Even in the earliest societies, even in the simplest tribal societies of modern times, there were probably occasions when the manner of organizing a hunt or a feast, a religious ceremony or a marriage, provoked criticism by some individual or social group. But in societies of this kind the scope of criticism is necessarily limited. The force of custom and tradition is very great, life is altogether precarious and difficult, and the established ways of behaving are not to be lightly altered or upset for fear of total disaster. It is only in societies which have become literate, possess economic reserves, have developed an urban life and in some measure a professional intellectual class, that any sustained criticism of the working of society is possible. In the West we like to think of classical Greece, and above all Athens in the fifth century B.C., as the shining example of a society in which, for the first time, free inquiry and criticism really flourished and became an accepted part of ordinary social life. There is some truth in this view, although it needs to be qualified in several respects. There have been other civilizations in which scientific inquiry and social criticism had an early flowering, and notably those of India and China. And on the other side, criticism in Athens was confined within a fairly small group of people, the subjects with which it dealt were restricted, and when the limits were exceeded it was punished. The condemnation of Socrates for corrupting the morals of the young (that is to say, for questioning very fundamental traditional ideas) is the most notorious instance. The example of Athens, in an idealized version, had its greatest effect in the later history of European thought.

The real beginnings of social criticism as a major influence upon human affairs are to be found in western Europe and North America in the eighteenth century; in a period which came to be called the age of enlightenment by contrast (in some respects, perhaps, a too simple contrast) with the dark ages of absolutism in government and in thought which had preceded it. Many influences contributed to the rise of a critical spirit. The ground had been prepared by the Reformation and the development of the Protestant sects, each with its own interpretation of the Christian religion and of the bearing of religion upon social conduct, as well as by the Renaissance, the revival of classical learning and the growth of humanism. The explosion of knowledge in the natural sciences, resulting from a greater freedom of inquiry and the use of experimental methods, and from the stimulus of industrial growth, encouraged the extension of this freedom and the application of these methods to the study of social life. Social and political changes worked in the same direction. A new intellectual class came into being, separated from the church. A new class of entrepreneurs and industrialists emerged, anxious to be free of feudal restraints and to gain access to the powers of government and administration. Democratic movements sprang up to demand the extension of political rights to the whole adult population. The growth of industry broke down old barriers and restrictions, but at the same time it created new problems: overcrowding, poverty, and insanitary conditions in the rapidly growing towns, changes in the family through the employment of women and children in factories, the need to expand education for industrial and commercial occupations, and to provide leisure activities for the urban masses.

It is hardly surprising, therefore, that in the latter part of the eighteenth century there should have appeared movements of social protest and social criticism on a scale hitherto unimagined. They were general throughout western Europe, but most intense at first in France. In the sphere of action their monument is the French Revolution, in the sphere of critical thought the great Encyclopaedia of Diderot and D'Alembert. The Encyclopaedia began modestly with a proposal to publish a French translation of an English encyclopaedia compiled by Ephraim Chambers, but it was transformed by Diderot into a critical survey of modern knowledge and its applications by many of the foremost thinkers and scholars of the time. The Encyclopaedia was intended to aid the progress of humanity by showing the ways in which the natural sciences had advanced, by attacking out-of-date ideas, and by applying the methods of science in the study of social and political questions. It brought together in a common enterprise writers, historians, philosophers and scientists, created a new body of ideas, and by its success diffused these ideas widely in France and abroad. As Voltaire later recorded more than 4000 copies of the first edition were sold, in spite of its high price, and among other things it produced a 500 per cent profit for the booksellers. The great achievement of the Encyclopaedists was to turn men's attention firmly upon their immediate environment, upon the worlds of science, industry and politics; and in this sense they were the progenitors of a vast undertaking of social criticism in France, by Saint-Simon and the early socialists, and by the social scientists, whether they were political economists or propounders of the new-fangled discipline of sociology.

In Britain the same ferment of ideas was occurring, though in a less dramatic manner. At first it was mainly the work of a small group of Scottish thinkers: David Hume, who advocated the application of experimental methods of reasoning to moral and political subjects, Adam Smith, who showed how it could be done in political economy, and such historians as Adam Ferguson and John Millar, who attempted to distinguish scientifically the stages of human progress, to show the character of social institutions at each stage, and to indicate what would be the institutions of the new industrial civilization. Somewhat later, the English Utilitarians pursued the attack on traditional ideas, criticizing the concept of natural law, endeavoring to make pleasure and pain as rigorously calculable as profit and loss, and contributing through the principle of the greatest happiness of the greatest number to the elaboration of a radical and democratic theory of society. Finally, the English socialists, like their French counterparts, took the new philosophical, economic and sociological ideas and worked them into a general criticism of capitalist society in the first few decades of the nineteenth century.

The development of social criticism in Germany was slower, and more philosophical in character, than it had been either in Britain or in France. Here it was the philosophers of history, and especially Hegel, who began the movement. Hegel, like the Scottish historians, attempted to define the stages of human progress, which he saw as the continuing growth of freedom. His philosophy was meant to be critical, both in the sense that he examined critically the institutions of earlier societies to discover what degree of freedom and rationality they incorporated, and also in the more important sense that he looked, in the contemporary society, for those new movements of thought which were destined to change and overthrow the old order of society. In his later years Hegel became more conservative in his social and political views, but his critical philosophy was continued in its radical form by the Young Hegelians in the 1830s and 1840s and it was turned more and more toward social problems. It was in this milieu that Karl Marx embarked upon his philosophical and historical studies, and it was in the Doctor's Club of the Young Hegelians in Berlin that he began to formulate his own explosive theories.

By the middle of the nineteenth century social criticism was firmly established in Europe, in a variety of forms. The early socialists, in France and Britain, had published their criticisms of the capitalist industrial system and had outlined the alternatives in programs of social reform or in speculative Utopias. The *Communist Manifesto* had appeared, in the year 1848, which saw the outbreak of revolutions throughout Europe. Socialist parties, trade unions, and co-operative societies had grown with amazing rapidity. Everywhere men were questioning traditional beliefs and the social rules by which they were expected to live.

The newer social sciences contributed largely to this movement of criticism, even when they were not directly associated with socialism. Political economists were led to examine the conditions of industrial workers, in the factories and in their homes, and some of them advocated sweeping reforms. The early sociologists dealt with a broader range of problems and raised questions about the character of government, the system of property ownership, the future of family life, and the social effects of religious and moral doctrines. Auguste Comte, in his *System of Positive Philosophy* argued that men's social life could no longer be guided and controlled by the Christian religion, which had presided over medieval Europe, and that a new scientific philosophy was needed in order to reshape political, economic and intellectual life. Herbert Spencer, the author of a sociological system which rivals that of Comte in its sweep, drew very different conclusions from his observation of the new social order. Devoted to *laissez faire,* and to the survival of the fittest as he conceived it, he saw no need for a single and exclusive doctrine to regulate social life and was content that religious and other creeds should also be in fierce competition with each other. He thought that this made for greater liberty, and he did not foresee the possibility that unregulated competition might end in monopoly. Nor was he very much concerned about the immediate economic consequences of the struggle for existence within society. Karl Marx, observing social life in still another fashion, recognized like Comte the significance of the growth of science and technology, but he saw their main effects in the formation of new social classes and the development of class conflicts; and he predicted the advent of an egalitarian society based upon co-operative production and blessed with affluence, while criticizing with the utmost bitterness the economic and political regime of capitalism.

Aside from these large-scale theories of society the social sciences provided materials for criticism in the numerous surveys of social conditions. The state of prisons, the health of the population in towns, the conditions of factory work (especially for women and children), poverty, unemployment, and ill-health among industrial workers, all became subjects for detailed investigation and exact description. As industrial development continued so the range of social problems widened, until in our own time the social sciences investigate a bewildering variety of matters, from industrial relations to divorce, from the needs of old people to the physical development of children.

Both social theories and social surveys added greatly to the fires of criticism which blazed up in the nineteenth century. To say this is not to claim that criticism is the sole or principal function, still less that it is the explicit intention, of all social scientists. Some of them have been social reformers and political radicals, but many others have regarded themselves first and foremost as impartial scientists, engaged in providing objective descriptions and explanations of social events. Yet it is difficult to separate entirely social science and social criticism. Most students of society have probably assumed that their science has some practical use, and have hoped that their discoveries might lead to some betterment of the human condition. Furthermore, even the most disinterested and objective description, when it deals with certain aspects of social life, implies or encourages a critical view. To depict faithfully and clearly, though dispassionately, gross inequalities, oppression, misery and suffering, is already a kind of criticism, or an incitement to it. To point to the causes may also be to show how they can be removed, and by whom. Thus, whether they will or not, the social sciences, social criticism and social reform have proceeded hand in hand.

The criticism which proceeded from socialists, reformers and social scientists was amplified by that of writers and journalists. Poets became revolutionaries, as did Heine and Shelley; novelists turned to the discussion of social issues—religious unbelief, the power of wealth, the struggle between classes, the rise of the working class, industrial and political conflicts—in what is called the naturalistic novel. Journals of opinion multiplied, the circulation of newspapers increased and the diffusion of criticism became wider and more rapid. From the end of the eighteenth century to the present time, there has been an ebb and flow of social criticism, varying in its tempo from country to country, varying also in the objects which have engaged its attention, but generally increasing in scale. Along with this and as one of its conditions has proceeded the steady growth of a secular intellectual class, which is devoted to the examination, and the criticism or defense, of the ways in which the institutions of our western societies function, and to the imagining of new institutions and new ways of living. Not only are we today unlike all earlier societies in our industrial development, our science and technology, and our wealth; we are unlike them too in our self-consciousness and self-criticism.

In the development of social criticism as I have sketched it, mainly in its European context, three principal features are observable. One is the succession of schools of thought which represent at different times the main weight of criticism of the established order of society, and which have an effect upon the way in which men regard even the more limited, detailed problems of their society. Such were, in France, the Encyclopaedists, the Saint-Simonians, the Marxists and the Catholic socialists of the 1920s and 1930s, the existentialists after 1945; in England, the Utilitarians, the early socialists, and the Fabians. In North America, although as we shall see social criticism was implanted in the society from the beginning, only later in the nineteenth century did it take shape in distinctive schools of thought, in agrarian socialism and populism, in pragmatism and social reform, and more ephemerally, in the campaigns of the muckrakers.

A second feature is the coalescence of different strands of social criticism, and of the counter criticism which it provoked, in broad movements of thought which could be identified as representing the "Left" and the "Right" in politics. This happened especially in the European countries in the second half of the nineteenth century and the early part of the present century. During this period the great ideologies of modern times were formed: socialism, communism, nationalism, conservatism, imperialism, fascism. These ideologies provided for their adherents a comprehensive view of society, a body of ideas and beliefs about social matters to which every particular criticism could be related. Some of them set out more deliberately than others to become all-embracing, and to bring every aspect of art, thought and behavior within their doctrinal scheme; but all of them tended to produce a more or less consistent view of what was wrong with society in general and how it should be remedied, and they were fairly clearly marked off from each other. Of course, not all social critics belonged wholeheartedly, or even at all, to one or other of these ideological camps. There were many who preferred to deal with social problems in a piecemeal fashion, and some who had their own independent nostrums: garden suburbs, or currency manipulation, or a religious revival. But still these ideologies dominated the scene in Europe.

In North America this was not the case. The dividing line between "Left" and "Right" was then, as it is today, much less clear, and there were many other divisions in society: in the United States, for example, between ethnic groups, and between regions—north, south, middle west and west; in Canada between the French and English speaking areas, and to some extent between geographical regions. Social criticism did not become consolidated, to the same degree as in Europe, in any dominant ideology; it has remained more diverse and sporadic, less coherent, and possibly less effective.

A third important characteristic of modern social criticism is its close association with protest movements, which range from mass campaigns such as Chartism or the civil rights movement to political parties organized on a permanent basis. Critical ideas are borne along by mass movements; at the same time they define and direct such movements. One consequence of this association is that the line between protest and criticism is sometimes difficult to draw. Protest movements may give rise to critical ideas as well as being inspired by them, and in a later chapter I shall discuss some recent movements from this point of view. But in the main I shall be concerned with social criticism as the work of thinkers who elaborate critical theories of society, and not as the mere expression, in any form whatsoever, of opposition to the established order.

In the world today there is everywhere a spate of social criticism; in the newly independent, economically under-developed nations, just as in the advanced industrial countries. The outpouring of books, journals and newspapers, the wide distribution of radio and television programs and of films, the tremendous expansion of high school and university education, ensure that ideas circulate quickly and reach a large and attentive public. Not all ideas are diffused everywhere with equal facility, and in some parts of the globe parochial orthodoxies may be upheld with the aid of censorship. But this is not the main feature of the present situation. It is rather that social criticism seems no longer to fall so clearly into the neat pattern of "Left" and "Right." The critic of society now often assails his own particular evil—the city, the mass society, technology, the bomb, the large organization, suburban life, the automobile, the mass media (in their entertainment role), racial discrimination—and does not attempt to link his criticism with any general conception of society as it is or as it might be. He may have some misty notion of an ideal society, but if so it is as likely to be a myth about the past as a vision of the future. Much social criticism is now devoted to the kind of problem which might be solved by bringing to bear some expert knowledge—for example, reducing the number of automobile accidents, or improving hospital care—while the main drift of social events is left to take care of itself. Or at the other extreme, the critic may condemn the whole social order—any social order—in a mood of anger and despair.

This situation is one which some recent writers have characterized as the "end of ideology"—a phrase which rings strangely if we consider how profoundly ideological have been the international conflicts of the past few decades. But if what is meant is that the great nineteenth century ideologies which divided societies internally have developed cracks and appear to be crumbling, and that they no longer exercise anything like their former sway over the minds of social critics, then the characterization may be accepted as plausible. The angry young men of the 1950s in Britain were not ideologists. They were not expounding a doctrine about how society could be reformed. They were complaining or denouncing; above all they were expressing some personal moral revolt. This is even more evident in some of the recent movements in North America; the most active participants in the civil rights movement and the student movement seem to be sceptical of, or hostile to ideologies, those "smelly little orthodoxies" as George Orwell once described them. They too seem to regard their criticism of society as the outcome of a very personal moral commitment, the sources of which, however, remain obscure.

Another way of describing the present nature of social criticism would be to say that the critics of whatever social order they are confronting no longer see one big social problem, for which there is one big solution. Instead, they see a succession of more or less unique situations, each of which requires the critic to take a moral stand, to commit himself, but only with respect to that particular situation. There is no rule for dealing with *all* situations. Our age, therefore, is certainly an age of criticism, but also one of exceptional confusion and disarray. How this condition came to be, and whether the present attitudes of social critics can be long sustained, I propose to examine in the following chapters.

CHAPTER 2

THE

PROGRESSIVE

ERA

The course taken by social criticism in North America was quite different from that in Europe, because the society itself was very different. The original colonies were established in part by religious dissenters, and in the course of time they attracted new groups of rebels against the religious and political powers of Europe. When, later, new orthodoxies began to emerge in the East, men were free to resume their criticism of society or to trek westward and begin again, and they did both these things. A new nation was finally created by the American Revolution, the first really successful assault upon the *ancien régime,* and one which in turn influenced the European revolutions. The leaders of this revolution debated at length and drafted in the Declaration of Independence and the Constitution statements on the rights of man and on the bases of political obligation which summarized some of the most radical political doctrines of the mid-eighteenth century.

Early in the nineteenth century it was recognized by European thinkers that a new kind of society had come into existence across the Atlantic. De Tocqueville, the most famous of these observers, in his *Democracy in America* (1st vol. 1835), characterized the United States as a democracy in two important senses: first, that political rights were widespread and not confined to the few, and secondly, that there was a tendency towards the equalization of the conditions of life. It was this equality, the absence of clearly defined orders and classes, which made possible the political democracy, the genuine participation of the mass of the people in government. Another feature which De Tocqueville noted was the pre-eminence of commercial and industrial activities, which, he considered, also made for equality since they did not give rise to privileged families which could maintain their position in society over the generations. Wealth was mobile and circulating; the prizes were open to all.

These observations may have been roughly true for the period up to 1835 when De Tocqueville published his book, but changes had already begun which provoked Americans themselves to criticism and proposals for reform. Emerson was writing in the early 1840s that "A restless, prying, conscientious criticism broke out in unexpected quarters. . . . We are to revise the whole of our social structure—the state, the school, religion, marriage, trade, science, and explore the foundations in our own nature."[1] In this there was some exaggeration. Much of the criticism emanated from New England; it was in large measure a renewal of the puritan ethic, in the form of the transcendental philosophy, and the expression of a desire to return to an earlier, simpler, supposedly more natural and purer state of society. It condemned the growth of economic inequality, the excessive devotion to success in trade, the abandonment of moral restraints in the accumulation of wealth.[2] It was highly individualistic, looking back to the age of the independent small property owner, and it called into being no major school of criticism or movement of reform, except in the anti-slavery movement. At the same time another stream of criticism, to which Emerson was also referring, came from the Utopian socialists. Many of the great European socialists—Robert Owen, Fourier, Cabet—established in America, either directly or through American disciples,

[1] R.W. Emerson, "Man the Reformer" (1841) in *Nature, Addresses and Lectures,* and "The New England Reformers" (1844) in *Essays, Second Series.* Excerpts from these two essays are reprinted in *The Era of Reform, 1830–1860* (New York, 1960) by Henry Steele Commager, who describes in his introduction the influence of the Transcendentalist philosophy, distilled in the writings of Emerson and Thoreau, upon the New England reformers. This theme is treated at length in Vernon L. Parrington's *Main Currents in American Thought, Vol. II, The Romantic Revolution in America, 1800–1860,* where the sources of transcendentalism are found in ". . . romantic Germany where the new idealism had quite routed the philosophy of sensationalism." "In essence," says Parrington, "this new transcendental faith was a glorification of consciousness and will. It rested on the rediscovery of the soul. . . ."

[2] Cf. Vernon L. Parrington, op. cit. p. 379, ". . . Emerson essayed to make clear to himself the function of transcendental criticism. . . . In the midst of a boastful materialism, shot through with cant and hypocrisy and every insincerity, fat and slothful in all higher things, the critic proposed to try the magic of sincerity, to apply the test of spiritual values to the material forces and mechanical philosophies of the times."

communities based upon their doctrines which took their place alongside the older religious communities, such as the Shakers, and the indigenous American ones of which the most famous was Brook Farm. Robert Owen, in addition, before he finally left America in 1845, tried valiantly to create a nationwide Workingman's Party, but without any success. The communities themselves were isolated from American society and were usually shortlived; even the more successful ones came to grief in the industrial expansion after the Civil War.

In retrospect, we can see many reasons for the failure of these social critics to inaugurate any distinctive and lasting school of criticism or widespread movement of reform. There were in the American society many problems and grievances, but few great issues. Slavery was the exception. Economic, and especially social, equality had still not been subverted. Above all, there was no such controversy and struggle over political rights as led to the growth of the socialist movement in Europe, for there were no major social groups, other than the slaves (and, of course, women), who were denied such rights. Even the industrial problems of Europe, and particularly of England, hardly existed, for America was still predominantly an agrarian and commercial country.

The decades following the Civil War were not an age of criticism, but one of exuberant optimism and of prodigious industrial and geographical expansion. In this period American society was transformed and the conditions were established for a new surge of criticism which, in its essential features, has persisted to the present day. The yeoman farmer finally disappeared before the advance of commercial agriculture. The towns grew rapidly with the development of industry; in 1860 the rural population was 25 million, the urban population only 6¼ million; by 1910 the rural population had doubled, but the urban population had multiplied almost seven times to nearly 42 million. In the middle of the nineteenth century there were hardly any millionaires; by the end of the century they were reckoned in thousands. The great trusts had come into existence, in railways, steel, banking and the meat packing industry. During the first part of the century there were few paupers or beggars; by the end of the century they swarmed in and around the great cities. In the 1880s mass immigration began to supply the additional workers needed by industry and brought new and staggering social problems in its wake; of education, poverty, and misgovernment.

The character of this period of American history is indicated very well by the intellectual pre-eminence which Herbert Spencer's social theory acquired. In England Spencer's views still had something of a radical character; in America they appeared as the perfect expression of the *status quo*. As an American wrote to Spencer in 1866: "The peculiar condition of American society has made your writings far more fruitful and quickening here than in Europe."[3] From the 1860s to the end of the century more than 350,000 copies of Spencer's books were sold in America, while they were for the most part ignored or dismissed in Europe. One of the founders of American sociology, C. H. Cooley, said of Spencer's influence: "I imagine that nearly all of us who took up sociology between 1870, say, and 1890 did so at the instigation of Spencer";[4] and a recent historian of ideas, Richard Hof-

[3] Henry Ward Beecher, quoted in Richard Hofstadter, *Social Darwinism in American Thought* (Boston, 1955) p. 31.

[4] Quoted in Richard Hofstadter, op. cit., p. 33.

stadter, in his book *Social Darwinism in American Thought,* has claimed that: "In the three decades after the Civil War it was impossible to be active in any field of intellectual work without mastering Spencer."[5]

The congruence between Spencer's ideas and the popular aspirations of post-bellum America is evident. Spencer was a fervent advocate of science and industry, an enthusiastic believer in progress (which would occur as a "beneficent necessity" if men would refrain from interfering with the natural course of social evolution), a champion of individualism and of the "survival of the fittest," and at the same time an admirer of representative government which he saw as the welcome concomitant of an industrial type of society. It would be hard to conceive a doctrine more in keeping with the individualistic, striving, competitive and commercial temper of American society in the latter part of the nineteenth century.

But the social changes of these decades following the Civil War led also to a revival of social criticism, which took shape initially in populism and agrarian socialism, mainly in the western states, and to a lesser extent in the cotton regions of the south. Its intellectual expression was largely in the tracts and journals of these political movements, but also in more substantial writings such as Henry George's *Progress and Poverty* (1879), Edward Bellamy's Utopian novel *Looking Backward* (1888), and H. D. Lloyd's *Wealth Against Commonwealth* (1894). By the middle of the 1890s populism had failed as a political movement, but many of the criticisms and reforms which it advanced were taken up in a new progressive movement, in which the organizations of industrial workers also participated, and which gave rise to a flood of socialist writ-

[5] op. cit. p. 33.

ings before the First World War. During this same period there was also a general reorientation of American social thought, which can be observed in three distinct spheres: (1) in social and political philosophy, (2) in the social sciences, and (3) in the works of publicists and journalists. The changes in philosophy, and to some extent in the social sciences, have been examined by Morton G. White in his book, *Social Thought in America,* and it is with these that I should like to begin.

Morton White singles out as the chief representatives of the new style of thinking, especially in social matters, John Dewey, Thorstein Veblen, Justice Holmes, Charles A. Beard, and James Harvey Robinson. Their characteristic doctrines—pragmatism, instrumentalism, institutionalism, legal realism, economic determinism—exhibit, he says, "striking philosophical kinships. They are all suspicious of approaches which are excessively formal; they all protest their anxiety to come to grips with reality, their attachment to the moving and the vital in social life."[6]

The most obvious common feature in the intellectual approach of these thinkers is their insistence upon the historical development of social phenomena. Holmes was concerned with the historical development of law in its social context, Dewey with that of morality (and eventually with the uses of history as a substitute for experiment in the social sciences). Veblen wanted to re-create economics as an evolutionary science, while Beard and Robinson aimed to establish history as a new science which would deal not with the formal legal relations between men, not with individuals, not with moral issues, but with underlying social processes. These concerns brought them close to the views of many German scholars at that time, especially

[6] Morton G. White, op. cit. p. 6.

the historical economists and the sociologists; and to Marxist ideas. Thus Robinson credited Marx with having originated the new outlook on history, and Beard, although his ideas had a basis in the argument of Madison that faction was the principal object of political studies and that the source of faction was property, was also much influenced by Marxism. In his *Contemporary American History, 1877-1913* (1914) he wrote: "The student of social and political evolution is concerned rather with the effect of . . . material changes upon the structure of society, that is, with the re-arrangements of classes and the development of new groups of interests, which are brought about by altered methods of gaining a livelihood and accumulating fortunes. It is this social transformation that changes the relation of the individual to the state and brings new forces to play in the struggle for political power."[7] From this it was only a step to the following description of the American scene about the end of the nineteenth century: the men of affairs and political leaders ". . . believed in the widest possible extension of the principle of private property, and the narrowest possible restriction of state interference, except to aid private property to increase its gains. They held that all of the natural resources of the country should be transferred to private hands as speedily as possible, at a nominal charge, or no charge at all, and developed with dashing rapidity."[8] Beard then drew the conclusion that this period represented a turning point in American society: "Deep underlying class feeling found its expression in the conventions of both parties, and particularly that of the Democrats, and forced upon the attention of the country, in a dramatic manner, a conflict between

[7] Charles A. Beard, op. cit. p. 32.
[8] op. cit. p. 53.

great wealth and the lower middle and working classes, which had hitherto been recognized only in obscure circles."[9]

Beard was not the only one among these thinkers who was led to recognize the rapid development of economic inequality and social differences, as well as increasing tension and conflict, in American society. Desiring to study social phenomena realistically, to grasp their historical development, and to deal in the manner of Hegel with what was new and growing in social life, they could hardly fail to be affected by the tumultuous and extraordinary changes in their society, and to become in some degree critics and reformers. The same influences and responses brought about great changes in the social sciences in this period, in ways that I shall discuss later. They also reached a much larger public, in a more direct fashion, through a different kind of critical writing, that of the muckrakers.

The title of "muckraker," borrowed from Bunyan's *Pilgrim's Progress,* was bestowed by President Theodore Roosevelt in a speech of 1906 which expressed his displeasure with those writers and journalists who devoted themselves too exclusively and too sensationally, as he thought, to the exposure of evils in American life, without taking due account of what was good and improving in it. The muckraking movement had begun in 1902—although it had precursors in the socialist and reformist writing of the previous decade—with the publication of articles by Lincoln Steffens on "the shame of the cities," and by Ida Tarbell on the history of the Standard Oil Company, in *McClure's Magazine.* Two factors determined the immense but transitory success of muckraking. One was simply the

[9] op. cit. p. 164.

need for reform in a society in which both wealth and poverty were assuming vast proportions, and in which city and even state government was deteriorating as a result of corruption. The other was the arrival of the inexpensive mass circulation magazine. *McClure's* had a circulation of nearly half a million by 1907, and other magazines, such as *Cosmopolitan, Everybody's,* and *Collier's,* which followed its example by lowering their prices and engaging in muckraking enjoyed a similar success.[10]

Muckraking was thus in one aspect a pioneer venture in the kind of sensational journalism which is now largely devoted to sex, crime and film stars. At its best, nevertheless, it was the work of serious reformers, whose writings were based upon extensive and careful research. The best known and one of the most scholarly of these journalists was Lincoln Steffens, and it is evident from his articles and from his *Autobiography*[11] how completely serious were his intentions. His first articles described the corruption of city government in St. Louis, Minneapolis, Pittsburgh, Philadelphia, and the attempts at reform in Chicago. Later, as he recounts in his autobiography, he became interested in the general process of corruption, which he saw as the replacement of democracy (that is, of representative government) by some kind of plutocracy; and in the causes which had operated to produce the identical phenomenon across America. He came to the conclusion at this time that the probable cause was not the dominance of business in American life, not even that of big business,

[10] For an account of the muckrakers and a good selection from their writings see Arthur and Lila Weinberg (editors), *The Muckrakers* (New York, 1961). See also the earlier account by John Chamberlain in *Farewell to Reform,* Chapter 4, "The Muck-rake Pack".

[11] *The Autobiography of Lincoln Steffens* (New York, 1931).

but the existence of "privileged business," and he regarded with approval the attempts of the reformers in Cleveland to do away with privileges by taking over the public service corporations and by the taxation of land values. Even so, he was not too hopeful, seeing the ideals of America on which reformers relied as "antiquated, dried-up, contradictory."[12] It is very doubtful indeed whether Lincoln Steffens ever arrived at a coherent view of the causes of corruption, or of the means to effect a cure. It is quite certain that he never communicated it to his mass readership.

The high point of the muckraking movement was reached in 1905-1906. This was the time when Upton Sinclair's novel, *The Jungle,* was published on the theme of the exploitation of workingmen, especially immigrant workers, by the meat packing trusts in Chicago. *The Jungle* recounts the agonies of a Lithuanian family, whose women are driven to prostitution, whose children die in the factory or on the streets, whose men are worn out by overwork, by starvation and by drink. A small part of the novel describes the unhygienic conditions of the packing industry and the evasion of health regulations, but this was the part which attracted by far the greatest amount of public attention. There was a storm of criticism and the sales of meat products plunged dramatically. That notorious character Mr. Dooley declared that he had become a vegetarian along with the President. As Upton Sinclair said later: "I aimed at the public's heart, and by accident I hit it in the stomach . . . I failed in my purpose. I wished to frighten the country by a picture of what its industrial masters were doing to their victims; . . . entirely by chance

[12] Lincoln Steffens, *Autobiography,* p. 494.

I stumbled on another discovery—what they were doing to the meat supply of the civilized world. . . ."[13] But the book had one immediate effect, the passage by Congress of the Pure Food and Drug Act, perhaps the only indisputable achievement of the muckrakers.

It is interesting to compare Upton Sinclair's novel with an English working-class novel which was written at the same time although it was not published until 1914; Robert Tressell's *The Ragged-Trousered Philanthropists*.[14] The major themes with which they deal are almost identical: the speeding up of work, the constant effort of the employers to reduce wages by getting rid of older skilled workers and employing younger unskilled ones, the indifference to the health and safety of workers, the domination of local politics (and their corruption) by the employers, the attempts of workers to form trade unions and the violent opposition of the employers. But there are absent in the English town described by Tressell the extremes of savagery and violence in the industrial life of Chicago; and there is absent too the oppressive sense of the hopelessness of the workingman's struggle. The hero of *The Jungle* eventually joins the socialists and he listens in the final scene of the novel to an orator declaring that: "Then will begin the rush that will never be checked, the tide that will never turn till it has reached its flood—that will be irresistible, . . . overwhelming—the rallying of the outraged workingmen of Chicago to our standard. . . . *Chicago will be ours!*" Yet the final impression we have is of a cry of defiance and despair rather than of hope. This contrast faithfully reflects—as we can see plainly from the van-

[13] Quoted in A. and L. Weinberg, op. cit. p. 205.
[14] New edition, presenting the complete original text (London, 1955).

tage point of the present time—the difference between a society in which there existed in the rising labor movement a secure basis for coherent social criticism, and one in which there was no such foundation and in which criticism remained fragmented and sporadic.[15]

The writings of the muckrakers were aimed very largely against the business and financial trusts, and against the corruption of politics. In this sense they represented a revival and continuation of the earlier populist literature attacking the "money power," and they were in accord up to a point with the criticisms expressed by the socialist movement. However, most of the muckrakers did not become socialists; they extended their investigations to other social problems of the time—the condition of Negroes, crime, prostitution, child labor, the influence of advertising—and in all these areas they helped to arouse a concern with social reform which flowed into the mainstream of the progressive movement. It was a further contribution by the muckrakers that their determined effort to get at the facts of American social life prepared the way for a new and more realistic kind of social science—the urban survey.

The development of social criticism in the United States as I have outlined it thus far shows some distinctive traits. American society was from the beginning modern, commercial and democratic. Social criticism found a congenial home here in a period when it was generally repressed in

[15] The reception accorded to the works of socialist thinkers at this time illustrates the same point. Louis Boudin's *The Theoretical System of Karl Marx* (1907), an outstanding exposition of Marxist economics, found no receptive audience. As Paul Sweezy has said (in D.D. Egbert and S. Persons, *Socialism and American Life*, I, p. 463): "Apparently American socialists were incapable of understanding Boudin; he remained a relatively isolated figure; more appreciated abroad than at home." W.E. Walling, one of the few serious thinkers in the Socialist party, a contributor to *The Masses*, and author of *Socialism as It Is* (1912), also received much less attention than he might have had in a different milieu.

the European countries. On the other hand there was less to criticize in American society at the outset. Social equality largely prevailed and the range of economic inequalities was limited. There were relatively few established positions of privilege and subordination. Government was in the main by discussion and by popular vote. In Europe, the social critics, having to deal with a past which was feudal and aristocratic, and with a present in which the new manufacturing class, sometimes in alliance with the old aristocracy, ruled over a population without political or social rights, were obliged to look to the future for a better organization of society; and they were encouraged to bring their critical ideas together in a general theory of social reform or revolution. In the United States, when the society began to change its character in the course of the nineteenth century, it was just as easy to look back to the early property-owning democracy as a golden age. Hence the ideas of the reformers in the middle of the century, and of the populists in the 1880s. Hence the resonance, even today, of appeals to some earlier and better condition of American democracy. Only toward the end of the century, when the industrial and urban transformation was seen to be irrevocable, did a school of thought emerge— that of the pragmatists—which was at all comparable in scope and coherence with the schools of criticism in Europe. Even then it appears that its ideas, like those of the muckrakers, were largely absorbed and diluted in the mainstream of American thought. According to Morton White, they had become ineffective by the end of the 1920s without having given rise to any new critical movement.

Among the critics of the progressive era the thinker who reveals better than any, perhaps, the diversity of sources which fed critical thought at the end of the nineteenth century, the connections which this thought had with populism on one side and with the social sciences on the other, the constant menace of incoherence and ineffectualness, is Thorstein Veblen. Veblen constructed his view of society from the ideas of the German historical economists, of Marx, of Darwin and the anthropologists, and to some extent from Dewey's pragmatism. He intended to give a realistic account of society, founded upon historical knowledge, which would be neither speculative nor romantic. In fact, one side of his own nature was incurably romantic, and the simple scheme upon which he based his account of social evolution is quite unhistorical. According to Veblen there are two principal stages of society, "savagery" and "barbarism"; the former peaceful, co-operative and industrious, the latter aggressive, competitive and acquisitive. Modern society is still "barbaric" in so far as these last characteristics predominate. The theme is expounded at length in *The Theory of the Leisure Class* (1899) which deals with acquisitiveness and parasitism, and in *Imperial Germany* (1915) which discusses aggressiveness, but it appears in most of his writings. What in Veblen's view would be the features of "savagery"—that is, of a good state of society—in the modern world? Sometimes Veblen writes like a populist, who sees the golden age in agricultural, rural America, before the "gilded age" of the great trusts and the financiers. One of his ideals was always the log cabin remote from the world. But then again he finds hope in the engineers, the practical makers of things, who are intelligent, peaceful and industrious, and he sketches the outlines of a society ruled by technologists, which is scarcely a Utopia for us today.

Most often, however, Veblen recoils from any expression of hope or condemnation (although his work is full of it) and insists that he is only describing realistically and analysing dispassionately the present state of society. It is all too plain that beyond his recognition of the new division in America between conspicuous wealth and crushing poverty, Veblen had no settled conviction about the direction that events were taking or about the direction that they should take. A brilliant, mordant critic; a provider of insights into the role of conspicuous consumption and waste in the struggle for prestige, and into the individual and social meaning of craftsmanship; he was neither a systematic thinker nor the founder of a school. It is for the temper of his mind, for his independent, awkward and eccentric character that he has been valued, not for his contribution to a new social theory. Much of his thought, and especially his emphasis upon the economic factors in social development, could be reabsorbed without too much difficulty into the conventional Marxism from which it came; his criticism of American society fitted easily into the ideas of the progressive movement. In the 1920s, with some reforms achieved, none of this proved strong enough to resist the drive of American society toward ever expanding production and ever increasing accumulation of wealth.

CHAPTER 3

FROM THE
JAZZ AGE
TO THE
GREAT CRASH

❀❀❀

The thinkers whose ideas I discussed briefly in my last chapter—Dewey, Veblen, Holmes, Beard and Robinson—were the most prominent instigators and representatives of a change in American social thought which began in the last quarter of the nineteenth century. One main source of this change was the transformation of American society itself; the rapid growth of industry and of towns, the appearance of great economic inequalities and the emergence of dissenting political movements such as populism. A second source is to be found in the academic world, where the influence of German universities and German thought introduced into the American social sciences the ideas of the historical economists and sociologists, and especially of those who became known as the "socialists of the chair"— the university teachers who had accepted, either wholly or in part, the Marxist social theory.

This development of ideas can easily be traced in the work of the early American sociologists. At first they were, as I noted previously, almost entirely under the sway of Herbert Spencer's theories. The most notable case was that of W. G. Sumner, who may be regarded as *the* founding father of American sociology, and who advocated extreme individualism, *laissez faire,* and the survival of the fittest, with an enthusiasm and intransigence surpassing that of Spencer himself. Sumner had his fervent disciples, and there were many others who adopted in a more moderate fashion Spencerian views. By the 1890s, however, there had arisen a strong movement of dissent, involving not only the socialists (inspired by Bellamy and H. D. Lloyd), but also some of the leading figures in American sociology, among them Ward, Ross and Small.

Two themes are prominent in the work of these dissenters and separate them clearly from the followers of Spencer. The first is their emphasis upon the part that the State should play in economic life, both in the stimulation of economic activity and in the regulation of competition. Lester Ward, for example, was an early advocate of State intervention, and he supported his case by the evidence of what was happening in the European countries, especially in Germany. Ross, who regarded himself as a disciple of

Ward, became an ardent reformer, a supporter of populism and a friend of the muckrakers, and moved still closer to a collectivist view.[1]

The second theme, best illustrated by the work of Albion Small, is the recognition of the growing importance of social classes in American society. It was a feature of Spencer's individualism, and still more of that of his American followers, that it set up a contrast between the solitary individual and the State while taking little account of intermediate bodies, except insofar as they were voluntary, contractual associations of the type of the business firm or the religious sect. The groups within society which individuals entered involuntarily, by their birth—and in particular social classes—received scant attention. Thus, when Sumner was provoked by the spread of socialist ideas and reforming movements, and by the growing expression of antagonism between classes, to write on the subject of class, he produced a book, *What Social Classes Owe to Each Other* (1883), in which he emphasized individual differences in capacity, equal opportunities, and the possibilities for mobility in American society. This was just at a time when class divisions were being more rigidly established and mobility was being curtailed.

Albion Small, who had studied in Germany and had been much influenced by the German Association for Social Policy in which liberal and socialist thinkers were active, was the first American sociologist to attribute a major importance to social classes and class conflicts and at the same time to give a sympathetic account of Marxist social theory. As the first head of a department of sociology, in

---

[1] See his *Sin and Society: An Analysis of Latter-Day Iniquity* (1907) in which he surveyed the revelations of the muckrakers and drew attention to the prevalence of social evils which were more serious in their effects and more difficult to grasp than was individual wrongdoing.

the University of Chicago from 1892, he was instrumental in spreading the ideas of European (and particularly German) social thinkers, and in associating sociology very closely with social criticism and reform. He was ready to argue, in his *General Sociology* (1905) that " . . . in all probability the sentimental philanthropic impulse has done more than the scientific impulse to bring sociology into existence. Men . . . so industriously advocated the improvement of social conditions that presently attempts to develop a scientific sociology became inevitable." It was Small's recognition of class inequalities and of the danger of serious class conflicts, coupled with his desire to find a peaceful solution through social reform, that stimulated the remarkable urban surveys carried out in Chicago in the 1920s and published in such books as Louis Wirth, *The Ghetto* (1928) and H. W. Zorbaugh, *The Gold Coast and the Slum* (1929).

The heyday of the progressive movement was the period from 1900 to 1914. During this time the socialists, the trade unions (whose membership grew in a decade from half a million to 2½ million), the pragmatists, the muckrakers, the new generation of economists and sociologists, seemed to be converging, and even uniting, in their criticism of American society. The movement was suddenly arrested by the war,[2] as was European socialism for a time, but unlike the latter it failed to regain its impetus in the postwar era. Men began to ask: What has become of the prewar radicals? Lincoln Steffens, reviewing the auto-

[2] See Randolph Bourne's comment on the war in his *Untimely Papers* (1919): "One has a sense of having come to a sudden, short stop at the end of an intellectual era." The war divided the radicals, some of whom supported America's entry into the war while others, including Bourne, bitterly opposed it. The liveliest of the radical journals, *The Masses,* was suppressed in 1917 for its opposition to the war.

biography of C. E. Russell in 1933 wrote that ". . . Muckraking hurt the muckrakers. One way or another they were all wounded by the work they did, by the sights they saw, by the fights they fought, by the defeats they suffered. Some became cynics, some 'tired liberals,' some dubious radicals, some unhappy fiction writers."[3]

The decade of the 1920s assumed a character quite different from that of its predecessor. Scott Fitzgerald gave it a name—the *Jazz Age*—and became its most brilliant interpreter. "It was characteristic of the Jazz Age," he wrote, "that it had no interest in politics at all." The criticism of American society now became a literary and cultural protest against a business civilization which was seen, however, as impregnable; the preferred method of protest, expatriation to Mexico, Paris or the Riviera, or an internal migration to Greenwich Village. Its tone was satirical. H. L. Mencken was in some ways a representative figure, with his contempt for both the business world and social reform, and his conviction that in America any serious cultural values were being crushed between the Rotarian and the peasant. But he pressed his satire to a condemnation of democracy itself, which he was disposed to see as the rule of the unenlightened mob through their vulgar and corrupt representatives. Arthur M. Schlesinger observes that: "What began as an alienation from business culture was ending in some cases as an alienation from democracy itself. And it was an alienation that provoked no exploration of social alternatives; for there seemed little point in seeking alternatives when the existing order seemed so

---

[3] In *The New Republic*, December 20, 1933. One important reason for the decline of radicalism was the violent campaign of repression directed against radicals after the war. See, on this subject, William Preston, Jr., *Aliens and Dissenters: Federal Suppression of Radicals 1903–1933*.

permanent."[4] The only conspicuous reforming movement of this time was that for Prohibition, a pseudo-reform of which Richard Hofstadter has well said that it was "a means by which the reforming energies of the country were transmuted into mere peevishness."[5]

The glorious spree of the Jazz Age ended with the great crash of 1929. In the years of economic depression which followed, when one quarter of America's workers were unemployed and many of those still employed were living in abject poverty, when the American dream had faded and the whole economic system appeared for a time to be on the brink of its final collapse, social criticism revived. But it did not recover either the vitality or the intellectual distinction of the progressive era. This decade of the 1930s has sometimes been portrayed as a "Marxist" period in American intellectual life, but the judgment calls for many qualifications. Certainly, Marxism was more frequently and extensively discussed in such liberal journals as *The Nation* and the *New Republic.* Yet it was not widely accepted; and above all, there was not created any significant body of Marxist social thought applied directly to American society and culture. Such patriarchs of progressive thought as Dewey and Beard were associated with the new radicalism, but their ideas were not drastically changed by the influence of Marxism, and Beard indeed was criticized for having abandoned much of his earlier economic interpretation of American history.[6] The writings of Veblen, which were assimilated into a socialist tradition of thought in other countries, met with a different

[4] Arthur M. Schlesinger, Jr.: *The Crisis of the Old Order, 1919–1933,* p. 150.

[5] Richard Hofstadter: *The Age of Reform,* p. 292.

[6] See the article by Max Lerner in *The Nation,* April 8, 1936.

fate in America. Veblen's conception of the role of the engineers in industrial society, as expounded by Howard Scott through the movement for technocracy, produced a minor stir in 1932 but the interest soon faded. More permanently, Veblen's economic writings influenced some of those who became members of Roosevelt's brain trust and architects of the New Deal; among them R. G. Tugwell, who adopted from Veblen the distinction between "industry" and "business" and saw as the great need of the times a reorganization of the industrial system which would introduce elements of economic planning and scientific management to modify and restrict the influence of purely financial and market considerations.

Among the younger intellectuals who were attracted by Marxism there were two who made distinctive contributions to a re-examination of social thought—Sidney Hook, especially in his *From Hegel to Marx,* and Edmund Wilson in *To the Finland Station.* In neither case, however, was there any attempt to relate Marxist theory to the particular conditions of American society or to the traditions of American social thought. So far as the political movements were concerned the writings of an English Marxist, John Strachey, and especially his book *The Coming Struggle for Power,* had probably a greater influence. Even in the intellectual sphere the American Marxists were not notably successful. Hook's writings were welcomed by a reviewer as "an index of the intellectual awakening in our higher social learning,"[7] but the awakening did not come. Edmund Wilson's study, which began as a series of articles in the *New Republic* in 1934, had turned into a highly critical account of Marxist theory by the time that it appeared as a

[7] *The Nation,* April 12, 1933.

book in 1940. It is noticeably less sympathetic to the Marxist method in social science than, for example, the work produced by E. R. A. Seligman, during the progressive era, on the economic interpretation of history.[8]

The vogue of Marxism in the United States was chiefly among the literary intellectuals, who seem to me to have continued, in another fashion, that alienation from American society which had begun towards the end of the nineteenth century. In the 1920s they protested against the business culture with satire and exile, believing it too strong to be overthrown. In the 1930s they attacked it more directly because it now seemed not only barbarous but also incompetent and doomed, while a viable alternative appeared to exist in the form of Russian communism.[9] An essay in *The Nation*[10] drew attention to this new direction in the literary world, claiming that there were two different pasts; one that of Lewisohn, Mencken and Carl Van Doren, in which "we observe the American artist gradually freeing himself from the limitations of puritanism . . . "; the other that of Granville Hicks and V. F. Calverton: "To them, of course, the villain is not the grim shadow of the Puritan but that coarser brute now generally known as the Spirit of Capitalism, and the meaning of our past is to be found not in the escape from conformity but in the gradual awakening of the social sense." The "proletarian novel"—exemplified by John Dos Passos' *U. S. A.* and James T. Farrell's *Studs Lonigan*—enjoyed much critical attention and acclaim, and the idea of a

[8] E. R. A. Seligman: *The Economic Interpretation of History* (1902; 2nd revised edition 1907).

[9] It was the literary intellectuals who published in 1932 *Culture and the Crisis*, a manifesto supporting the communist candidates for the Presidency.

[10] "The Usable Past", *The Nation*, February 14, 1934.

proletarian culture inspired the activities of the John Reed clubs.

The social thinkers, on the other hand, by the very nature of their studies, were led to examine more closely what changes were actually occurring in American society and in the outlook of the American people, and their theories were more realistic and less extreme than the visions of the writers and journalists. There is an excellent example in the surveys by Robert and Helen Lynd of a small town in the middle west, which they called *Middletown*. The first survey was conducted in 1924-1925, the second in 1935 to observe the effects of the economic depression in the town. The Lynds were certainly social critics, and they were very much aware of the inequalities of wealth and power between social classes in American society. They regarded as one of the basic distinctions in Middletown that between the "business class" and the "working class." In describing the experiences of the town during the depression years they noted the growth of tension and suspicion between these two classes, but they summed up the reactions of workers in the following way: ". . . this fear, resentment, insecurity, and disillusionment has been to Middletown's workers largely an *individual* experience for each worker and not a thing generalized by him into a '*class*' experience. Such militancy as it generates tends to be sporadic, personal and flaccid; an expression primarily of personal resentment rather than an act of self-identification with the continuities of a movement or of rebellion against an economic status regarded as permanently fixed." And in the final chapter of the book they speak of Middletown facing both ways—into the past and into the future—and of continuing its course of reluctant adaptation and expediency.

The experiences of great industrial cities were not, of course, the same as those of Middletown, but they were closer to these, I think, than they were to Marxist ideas of the class struggle. The survey of Middletown thus provides an indication of why Marxism remained so much an affair of small political sects, and why, although it pervaded the intellectual atmosphere, it did not create a new and effective school of social criticism.

The major works of social criticism in the 1930s were not Marxist. One of the most influential was the book by Adolf Berle, Jr. and Gardiner Means, *The Modern Corporation and Private Property* (1932). Berle and Means drew attention to two important changes in the American economic system: (1) the concentration of industrial production in a relatively small number of giant corporations, and (2) the separation between the ownership and control of industry. As to the first, they observed that the 200 largest non-banking corporations controlled in 1930 about one-half of the total non-banking corporate wealth of America. They expected this process of concentration to continue. As to the second, they noted that the diffusion of ownership through the growing numbers of stockholders meant that the policy of each corporation was determined by a few men, the directors, who were not its owners. Some 6000 men, they concluded, virtually controlled the American economy. From this analysis, Berle and Means went on to argue that competition and the operations of the market no longer regulated the economy as a whole. The giant corporation was less like an economic unit of the kind familiar in classical economics, than it was like a nation. The corporation managers of the future would have to function "more as princes and ministers than as promoters or merchants." Two conclusions were drawn from this:

first, that the economy as a whole needed to be regulated by the state, and secondly, that in this regulation a responsible business community, aware of its new position and powers, should play an important part.

What Berle and Means advocated was a system of "managed capitalism," which would take account of the profound changes in the American economy, but would not seek to bring about any profound changes in American society. It expounded a managerial and technological, rather than an ideological view. In this it resembled another book, otherwise very different, which was widely read in the 1930s, Thurman Arnold's *The Folklore of Capitalism* (1937). Arnold was chiefly concerned to show that the way in which the economic system had been described did not correspond with its actual modern working, and so to expose the uselessness of the conventional ideas about it. At the same time he exposed some of the ideas of earlier progressive thinkers about how it could be reformed. In his own attitude, technique, organization, and much that would nowadays be called "social engineering"—as opposed to utopian social planning—had pride of place.

This kind of social criticism, and the American experience of the New Deal, were eventually brought together in a new social theory in James Burnham's *The Managerial Revolution* (1941). Burnham accepted the view that *laissez-faire* capitalism could not survive, but he rejected the Marxist theory that it would be followed by socialism; that is, by a form of society in which industrial property would be collectively owned, and in which social classes would cease to exist. In his view, there was no sign at all that this was coming about. It was much more probable that capitalism would be replaced by a managerial society, in which a class composed of scientists, technologists, and the organizers of production would rule. This theory incorporates a good part of Veblen's ideas, as well as those of Berle and Means, and at the same time it reflects some of the consequences of the New Deal administration.

During the 1930s the social sciences were only slightly affected by Marxism. On the contrary, it might be said of this period that it was a time when the post-Marxian European thinkers—especially Pareto and Max Weber—were being discovered in America. There was a growing interest in the pure theory of society, and in many intellectual circles a declining interest in social criticism. What has been seen subsequently as the acceptance of Marxism was often enough only the expression of a general sympathy with socialism, or more specifically with the economic and social policies of the U.S.S.R. Lincoln Steffens ended his *Autobiography* of 1931 with some chapters of praise for Russia, and declared in his speeches that "all roads in our day lead to Moscow"; but he was nothing of a Marxist and what he praised was chiefly the resolute implementation of an economic plan. Bellamy's novel *Looking Backward*, a very American and quite un-Marxist exposition of socialism, enjoyed a considerable revival. But few intellectuals actually joined the Communist Party or the Socialist Party, and fewer still remained within them for any length of time.

The resurgence of radicalism in the 1930s was inspired by the domestic events of the depression and also by international events—by the world economic crisis, and in particular by the rise of national socialism in Germany. The radicalism of the intellectuals, as revealed for instance by the tone of the liberal journals, became pronounced after 1932 when the national socialist threat had been plainly shown.[11] It would not have been surprising if in these conditions Marxism had had a wide appeal. The gulf between classes in America had never appeared greater, and capitalism throughout the world seemed to be breaking down in a general crisis of the kind which Marx, and after him Lenin, had predicted. There was a dramatic confrontation between the old order of society and the new in the opposition between national socialism and the international communist movement, culminating in the Spanish Civil War. The influx into America of intellectuals who were refugees from national socialism brought with it something of the urgency of the social struggles in Europe, as well as the ideas of thinkers who had long been Marxists.

The radical revision of ideas about Russia was provoked by these two series of events, domestic and foreign. In the context of the depression Russia appeared as a society which had solved the problem of economic crises by means of rational planning and had been able to introduce welfare services superior to those in the capitalist countries; in the international context Russia appeared as the center of determined resistance to national socialism. Such reappraisals were not uniquely American; the English Fabians, Sidney and Beatrice Webb, were converted to an enthusiastic partisanship which they announced in a massive study

[11] A selection of articles from *The New Republic* has been published under the title *The Faces of Five Decades* (edited by Robert B. Luce); but because it concentrates upon essays written about individuals it fails almost entirely to convey the radical outlook of the journal in the period 1932–36. There is an anthology from *The Nation* under the title *One Hundred Years of The Nation*, edited by Henry M. Christman, which likewise fails to convey the changes in outlook and tone which occurred from one decade to another. The period of the muckrakers and the progressives is not represented at all, and the 1930s only very inadequately. There are, however, four informative introductory essays; one by the present editor, and three others on "*The Nation:* Its Role and History".

entitled *Soviet Communism: A New Civilization.*[12] Most of the American intellectuals were still critical of certain aspects of Soviet society—as were the Webbs—and their criticisms grew in volume after the beginning of the Moscow trials; but the impact of Soviet communism continued to be strong.

In the conditions of the 1930s the surprising fact is that the influence of Marxism, or of any socialist ideas, was so slight, and that the radical movement had so little success either in approaching its immediate objectives or in establishing itself as a permanent force in American politics. The need for a "third party" was often asserted, and from 1933 onwards there were many attempts to create a new radical party, inspired largely by the success of the Farmer-Labor Party in Minnesota and of the Progressive Party in Wisconsin. These efforts culminated in a Third Party Conference in Chicago in July 1935,[13] but they proved vain.

The absence of a broad radical movement—the place of which was taken by sporadic protests and revolts among students, farmers and the unemployed—and the inability to work out an effective social theory, were related. Some critics themselves drew attention to the gulf which existed between revolutionary intellectuals and the great majority of the population; and one such critic, discussing the so-called "proletarian novel," observed: "While novelists, in the main, fought shy of the proletarians, critics in some cases welcomed the new literary credo. . . . In Greenwich Village the revolution seemed about to burst forth at any moment. . . . After election day, when noses were counted, it was discovered that about one hundred thousand Ameri-

---

[12] Published in 1935.
[13] See the report in *The Nation,* July 24, 1935.

cans had voted red—one fourth of one per cent of the electorate. The millions of unemployed, the dispirited of the breadlines and flophouses, had voted for either Hoover or Roosevelt. Even the mild Socialist program suffered overwhelming defeat. . . . After three years of provocative and bloody tactics in which demonstrators and strikers had been clubbed in scores of American cities . . . the masses stubbornly voted Republican or Democratic."[14] This social isolation of the intellectuals was an important element in producing the diversity of views and the sectarian struggles which flourished among them. As John Chamberlain wrote of the earlier progressive era in his *Farewell to Reform*, which he published just in the early 1930s when radicalism was apparently on the upsurge again: "Class distinctions had not been drawn in hard and fast lines: because of this the prophets of discontent sounded a Babel of conflicting tongues."[15] This is just as true, and perhaps even more true, of the 1930s. Such investigations as the Lynds' *Middletown in Transition*[16] show how little class divisions had been consolidated or recognized, and how feeble was the development of working-class consciousness; their findings confirm in detail the evidence from elections and from the outlook and activities of the trade unions in this period. As to the "conflicting tongues," they are only too apparent in the rapid circulation of new creeds— technocracy, social credit, semantics, among others—and in the bitterness of sectarian strife which the doctrinaire intolerance of the Communist Party intellectuals made still more acute. A particular illustration is to be found in the response to Upton Sinclair's campaign for the governor-

[14] Charles Y. Harrison in *The Nation*, March 22, 1933.

[15] John Chamberlain, *Farewell to Reform: The Rise, Life and Decay of the Progressive Mind in America*, p. 42.

[16] See above, p. 40.

ship of California[17]—EPIC, or End Poverty in California—which a number of radicals attacked in violent terms as an abandonment of socialism,[18] even though one of Sinclair's major themes was the development of co-operative production units, an idea which is entirely socialist and which had the merit at that time of expressing the aims of some real social movements.[19]

Many radical intellectuals became discouraged, and withdrew, either then or later, from any political involvement. Their retrospective judgment upon the decade of the thirties is well represented by Alfred Kazin's sad and disabused account of his early beliefs, in his autobiography *Starting Out in the Thirties*. Others became, in the later 1930s, supporters of the New Deal, as some of their predecessors, the progressives of the 1900s, had become supporters of Theodore Roosevelt. It was not, I think, that the New Deal held out the promise of massive social reforms, nor that it was successful in promoting large-scale economic recovery before increasing war production came to its aid. But it engendered a new optimism, it reawakened for a time the populist sentiment of the beginning of the century, and it offered at least the hope of a more efficiently managed economy. Moreover, so far as any new and potent ideas made their appearance in this decade they were those which concerned the institutions and problems of a technological and managerial society, and they flourished, even if they were not invented, in the circle of the

[17] See his pamphlets *I, Governor of California* and *How I Ended Poverty in California*.

[18] A reviewer in *The Nation*, February 21, 1934 began thus: "Upton Sinclair, at fifty-five, after professing and preaching socialism most of his life, has turned to the right." See also the article by Carey McWilliams in *The New Republic*, August 22, 1934.

[19] For example, the production units formed by the unemployed in Dayton, Ohio. See *The Nation*, April 19, 1933.

New Deal brain trust. Above all, however, there was no social movement which provided a real alternative to the New Deal. The situation was entirely different in most of the European countries. There, large working-class parties existed, already socialist if not Marxist in doctrine. The revival of Marxist thought was more profound and had a greater effect. Even though socialist parties did not gain power, did not remain long in power, or were defeated and repressed, they conserved or increased their strength sufficiently to ensure a new wave of radicalism after 1945.

For other reasons the state of affairs in the U.S.A. and in Canada differed greatly in the 1930s. Before this time there had been little effective social criticism in Canada. There were populist movements, largely influenced by those in the U.S.A., at the turn of the century; and there was some militant trade unionism. But there was no systematic critical study of the society, and no social thought which was not almost entirely derivative. Canada had a small population dispersed over a vast territory and lacked the great urban centers in which intellectual life might flourish. English-speaking Canada had been settled by loyalists rather than dissenters, while the French-speaking area reproduced and even exaggerated the social institutions of the *ancien régime* in France. The society as a whole was conservative, not radical; in intellectual matters it was largely dependent upon other societies. It was not self-critical.

The lack of an indigenous tradition of social criticism is illustrated very well by the fact that one of the most profound problems of Canadian society—the relations between English- and French-speaking Canada—was only studied with any thoroughness, up to the 1930s, by foreign scholars. The most important of the early studies is that published in 1906 by a French political scientist, André Siegfried, which appeared in an English translation in 1907 with the somewhat misleading title *The Race Question in Canada*.[20] A generation later a revealing study of the changes in French-Canadian society was made by an American sociologist, Everett Hughes, and was published in 1943 under the title *French Canada in Transition*.

These circumstances began to change in the 1930s. The economic depression had consequences here which were far different from those in the United States. One vital difference was that no doctrines or policies resembling those of the New Deal were adopted wholeheartedly by the established Canadian parties. This allowed, and even obliged, social criticism and protest to take shape in new political movements, especially in the western provinces where there was already a tradition of agrarian radical movements. The 1930s thus saw the creation of two new parties, Social Credit in Alberta and the Co-operative Commonwealth Federation in Saskatchewan. The former had affinities with the populist movements of the 1880s in the U.S.A., but adopted its doctrines from the writings of the currency reformer Major Douglas, whose ideas were also much discussed in the United States in the early 1930s. The C.C.F. has been described by one writer as the lineal descendant of the recurring farmers' movements in western Canada, and particularly of the United Farmers' movement between 1910-1919,[21] but it was successful in bringing together a number of different groups—farmers,

[20] The title, however, follows Siegfried's own unsatisfactory use of the term "race." A new edition of the book, with a useful introduction by F. H. Underhill, has recently been published in the Carleton Library (McClelland and Stewart, 1966).

[21] Dean E. McHenry, *The Third Force in Canada: The Co-operative Commonwealth Federation 1932–1948.*

industrial workers, intellectuals, and a small group of Members of Parliament[22]—to form a political party which declared itself in favor of socialism,[23] and which modeled itself in some degree upon the British Labour Party. These two movements, and particularly the C.C.F., established in North America new social doctrines, and they diffused in due course a more critical attitude toward Canadian institutions and beliefs. In my view, the development of critical social thought in Canada since the war can be traced on one side to these political movements, and on the other to the renaissance of French-Canadian culture.

[22] The C.C.F. was founded at the Western Labor Conference held in Calgary, July 1932, which was attended by some hundred delegates representing farmer, labor and socialist organizations in the four western provinces, as well as the Ginger Group of M.P.'s and the League for Social Reconstruction.

[23] The Regina Manifesto, adopted at the first National Convention (1933) states: "We aim to replace the present capitalist system, with its inherent injustice and inhumanity, by a social order from which the domination and exploitation of one class by another will be eliminated, in which economic planning will supersede unregulated private enterprise and competition, and in which genuine democratic self-government, based upon economic equality will be possible."

CHAPTER 4

THE

NEW

RADICALISM

The cycle of social criticism in the United States during this century has followed something like a generational pattern, with the peaks occurring in the 1900s, in the 1930s and again in the 1960s. But this regularity is only one aspect of a complicated movement. Another aspect is the changes in the character of social criticism in each of these periods which resulted from the condition of American society, its prevailing ideas, and its relations with the rest of the world.

The progressive era at the beginning of the century was followed by the Jazz Age; pleasure-seeking, light-hearted, at least on the surface, and relatively uninterested in politics. The reforming movement of the 1930s was followed by the sombre and tormented era of McCarthyism, overflowing with political passion.[1] The differences are explicable in part by the changed state of the world and of the United States' place in it. After the First World War there was no immediate new alignment of opposed great powers, and the United States was still not totally involved in world politics. After the Second World War the United States was deeply involved, and had to confront another great power—Russia—which had considerably extended its sphere of influence and directly challenged the American way of life. This was clearly not a time for carefree frolics, even if men's spirits had not already been depressed by the terrible discovery of the atomic bomb.

But McCarthyism also exemplified something more permanent in American life. It was itself a form of social criticism and dissent, though not of an intellectual kind. Indeed, it was rabidly anti-intellectual. In some ways it may be viewed as the Prohibition movement of the 1950s, expressing the same moralizing, censorious and peevish attitudes, and having the same irrelevance to the major problems of the time. It exhibited, as did Prohibition, that strain of intolerance which many observers have found in

[1] It is a commonplace observation that there was little interest in radical politics in the early 1950s. Dwight Macdonald, for instance writes in his *Memoirs of a Revolutionist:* "We are less interested today in radical politics—that is, parties, programs, ideologies that assume a radical (in the sense of going to the roots) reconstruction of the old order. Indeed, one might almost say we aren't interested at all, and that this kind of politics no longer attracts intellectuals . . ." (p. 4). It would be wrong to conclude, however, that the age was therefore "unpolitical"; it was simply a time in which the political offensive was taken by thinkers and politicians of the right.

American life,[2] running alongside and contradicting the tradition of free inquiry and criticism. Only McCarthyism was more intolerant, more virulent and certainly more dangerous to liberty than was Prohibition.

Other elements besides the uncertainties of the international situation and the propensity to intolerance (which itself needs to be explained) contributed to the temporary success of McCarthyism. One of these was perhaps the prevalence of "status anxiety," which Richard Hofstadter has examined closely in an essay dealing with the "radical right." The "rootlessness and heterogeneity of American life, . . . its peculiar scramble for status and its peculiar search for secure identity," have given rise, he argues, to a form of status politics which tend "to be expressed more in vindictiveness, in sour memories, in the search for scapegoats, than in realistic proposals for positive action."[3] Another element was the quiescence of the radical intellectuals, which seems to have resulted from a loss of confidence and excessive feelings of guilt about their earlier Marxist, or even liberal, views, when the enormities of Stalinist rule in Russia and in eastern Europe began to be revealed.

Nevertheless, a revival of self-confidence and of critical thought began to take place in the 1950s, this time not among the philosophers or historians, but among the social scientists and particularly the sociologists. The leading figure in this movement was C. Wright Mills. As a radical critic of American society Mills most closely resembled Veblen, although he was both less original and more systematic as a thinker. His major purpose, as he often said,

[2] See, for example, S. M. Lipset, "The Sources of the 'Radical Right'", in Daniel Bell (editor), *The Radical Right*, pp. 316–320.

[3] Richard Hofstadter, "The Pseudo-Conservative Revolt", in Daniel Bell (editor), op. cit., pp. 83, 85.

was to revive a classical, largely European tradition of sociological thought, which had been created above all by Marx and Max Weber, and which treated large-scale social and historical problems.

The subjects which Mills tackled belong clearly to this tradition. He was interested especially in the massive changes which had taken place in the social structure, and especially the class structure, of the United States since the beginning of the nineteenth century, and in the political consequences of these changes. One of his earliest books, *The New Men of Power: America's Labor Leaders* (1948) dealt with the evolution of the American working class and with the circumstances which had made the leaders of American trade unions aspirants for a place in the national elite rather than critics of the economic and social system of American capitalism.

Mills' next book, *White Collar* (1951), examined the American middle classes and if it did not inaugurate, it certainly re-invigorated and advanced the debate among social scientists upon the significance of the great expansion of middle-class occupations in the industrial societies. Most Marxists, following Marx, had argued that the middle classes would gradually decline as capitalism developed —that they would be crushed out of existence between the large capitalists on one side and the wage earners on the other. The critics of Marxism observed that although the "old" middle classes—the independent small producers, tradesmen and professional men—might be declining in numbers, the "new" middle classes of white collar, technical and professional employees were increasing very rapidly and were assuming a similar position in society. Britain, which Napoleon referred to as a nation of shopkeepers, had become by the middle of the twentieth century, as one commentator put it, a nation of clerks. The change was even more striking in the United States which, in the early nineteenth century, had been much more preponderantly than any European country a society made up of small property owners—farmers, traders and manufacturers. At that time some 80 per cent of the employed white population were independent, self-employed producers; by 1940, only 18 per cent were self-employed. Mills documented this change, but he did not accept the view that the new middle classes fitted exactly into the place of the old. On the contrary, he thought that the prevailing ideology, with its emphasis on independence, individualism and mobility, which fitted well the small-propertied world of the early nineteenth century, was only a mystification in the conditions of the mid-twentieth century when most Americans, as he put it, had become "hired employees." The new middle classes do not have either the security or the deep convictions of the old. As Mills says: "The new Little Man seems to have no firm roots, no sure loyalties to sustain his life and give it a center." And again: "Among white-collar people, the malaise is deep-rooted; for the absence of any order of belief has left them morally defenseless as individuals and politically impotent as a group." This is a theme in recent social criticism to which I shall return.

In the third of the books which he devoted to the American class structure, *The Power Elite* (1956), Mills examined the upper class in the United States. This was the book which created the greatest stir, largely because it appeared to re-state and provide evidence for a view which socialists had been expounding ever since the 1880s; namely, that the United States, in spite of its democratic forms and its "classless" ideology, had in fact a ruling class.

But this was not quite what Mills was saying. Early in the book he sets out several alternative conceptions of the nature of elites (which he also refers to as the "upper stratum" and the "higher circles"), but he does not examine closely the notion of a ruling class; and in a later chapter where he expounds his general view of the power elite he rejects explicitly the Marxist idea of a ruling class based upon property ownership in favor of the concept of elites, which he defines as those groups of people who actually exercise power, no matter how they have got into a position to do so. "'Ruling class,'" he writes, "is a badly loaded phrase. 'Class' is an economic term; 'rule' a political one. The phrase 'ruling class' thus contains the theory that an economic class rules politically. That short-cut theory may or may not at times be true, but we do not want to carry that one rather simple theory about in the terms that we use to define our problems. . . . Specifically, the phrase 'ruling class,' in its common political connotations, does not allow enough autonomy to the political order and its agents, and it says nothing about the military as such."[4] In accord with this conception Mills distinguishes three important elites in the United States—the political leaders, the big business executives, and the military chiefs—and he goes on to claim that the three groups have coalesced in a power elite which makes all the important decisions affecting American society, so far as such decisions are deliberately taken at all. It is not made quite clear just how this power elite has become so powerful and so unified. Is it the sheer growth in the size of economic, political and military organizations which has removed them from any possible control by their ordinary members? Does the state of international conflict encourage or make essential the alli-

[4] op. cit., p. 277 footnote.

ance between politicians, the military, and the producers of colossally expensive weapons? One thing is clear from Mills' account; namely, that the power elite in the United States is not a ruling class in the sense of a stable and continuing group which pursues a settled policy. Among the principal accusations that Mills levels against it is precisely that it is irresponsible and does not know where exactly it is going. Some of his criticisms here rejoin those of the conservative critics of American society (whose ideas I shall be considering later), who suggest that while the United States has a highly privileged upper class it does not now, if it ever did, have a ruling class in the sense of one which can authoritatively define and establish national standards of behavior. It is interesting, for example, that Mills insists strongly upon the influence which an independent and respected body of high civil servants might have in limiting the irresponsibility of the power elite.[5]

The main distinction which Mills draws in this book is not one between classes, but between the power elite and the masses. He sees America as being rapidly transformed into a mass society; that is, a society in which a mass of unrelated individuals lose any effective means of criticism or influence and become easily manipulable by their rulers. His suggested remedies are not put in Marxist terms, involving changes in the class structure (although this is sometimes implied), but rather in terms of the need to re-establish or re-animate voluntary and local organizations, through which the individual might regain a genuine control over decisions of public policy. This criticism has, obviously, a wider bearing than upon North American society alone. Its relevance to other industrial societies made Mills' book influential in western Europe and even

[5] op. cit., pp. 237–241.

in the Soviet countries, since its publication coincided almost exactly with the post-Stalin thaw and with the beginnings of a critical assessment of bureaucracy in socialist societies. In North America Mills' observations on mass society took their place in a stream of criticism concerning the effects of large-scale organization, and the changing American character, some of which I shall consider shortly.

There is another feature in Mills' studies of the class structure which reflects very clearly their North American origin. After his first book, Mills had little to say about the labor movement, and especially about its part in producing any social reforms. In discussions with European social critics he was apt to treat as pure romanticism their view that the working-class movement was still the principal source and agency of criticism, protest and reform.[6] He was strongly influenced in this attitude by the circumstances of the United States, where there has never been a politically independent working-class movement on the European scale, and where the experiences of radical thinkers ever since the 1930s must tend to produce scepticism about the likelihood of any such movement developing. But in that case, where did Mills look for a renewal of social criticism and of the progressive movement? The answer is not altogether clear. Mills was not a rebel without a cause, but his cause was formulated in very general and abstract terms, and it was not obviously associated with any actual social movement. He was also a fairly representative

---

[6] For example: ". . . what I do not quite understand about some New Left writers is why they cling so mightily to the 'working class' of the advanced capitalist societies as *the* historic agency, or even as the most important agency, in the face of the really impressive historical evidence that now stands against this expectation. Such a labor metaphysic, I think, is a legacy from Victorian Marxism that is now quite unrealistic." "The New Left" in *Power, Politics and People* (edited by Irving L. Horowitz), p. 256.

critic of the mid-twentieth century in that he could sympa-
thize with the state of mind of the rebel who was obscurely
revolted by the conditions of social life, yet was unable to
conceive with any clarity a possible alternative or a course
of action. As he wrote in the introduction to *White Collar:*
"The uneasiness, the malaise of our time, is due to this
root fact: in our politics and economy, in family life and
religion—in practically every sphere of our existence—the
certainties of the eighteenth and nineteenth centuries have
disintegrated or been destroyed and, at the same time, no
new sanctions or justifications for the new routines we live,
have taken hold. So there is no acceptance and there is no
rejection, no sweeping hope and no sweeping rebellion.
There is no plan of life."

In an earlier period of radicalism Veblen had been capable, on occasion, of looking hopefully into the future to a
time when the engineers might reorganize society in ac-
cordance with their ideals of craftsmanship and efficiency.
Mills was more pessimistic, not because he was personally
unsure about the objectives of a radical movement, but
because he could not see in the industrial societies, and
particularly in the United States, any group which had
unmistakably the vision and the energy to resist the drift
toward catastrophe. In the end he decided that the best
hope lay with the intellectuals, as a possible force to bring
about radical changes; and especially with the younger intellectuals and students who, as he pointed out, had recently taken the lead in movements of revolt, in western
countries as well as in the Soviet societies and in the third
world. This conclusion led him directly to a critical examination of what he called "the cultural apparatus" in the
modern world, upon which he was still engaged when he
died; and in the first place to a study of the role of the

social sciences which he published in 1959 as *The Sociological Imagination.*

If the intellectuals were to assume this important role as
the pioneers and leaders of social change, then it was plain
to Mills that social scientists, because of their professional
concern with the ways in which societies are organized,
maintain themselves and change, should play a leading
part in the movement. Unfortunately, they appeared very
ill-equipped to do so in the United States. According to
Mills, the classical manner of social thought and inquiry,
which directed its attention to large public issues and communicated its findings in a language which was intelligible
and even agreeable to the educated public, had been given
up in favor of a new style of social science, principally
though not entirely among the sociologists. This new style
consisted, on one side, in the elaboration of concepts and
categories, without much reference to the problems or investigations in which such concepts might serve a purpose;
and on the other, in the refinement of methods of investigation. As a British sociologist remarked, parodying
Churchill, the plea of the methodologists seemed to be:
"Give me a job and I will spend the rest of my life polish-
ing the tools." The results of these two branches of sociology were presented, more and more frequently, in an im-
penetrable jargon, to which an indignant American critic
gave the name of "socspeak."

The Sociological Imagination was a sustained criticism
of these tendencies, which Mills saw as a means of escape
from responsibility and commitment; and an impassioned
plea that social scientists should return to the study of the
great problems which agitated, confused or frightened
men in the modern world. The argument of the book was
well received, though with some reservations, in Europe as

well as in the United States. It appeared at a time when there was in most countries a revival of left-wing social thought, and—in the United States—the emergence of a variety of protest movements whose contribution to social criticism I shall be considering later. Mills' ideas were in part a response to the revival of a radical student movement, and at the same time they were accepted as expressing the concerns and beliefs of the students and the younger intellectuals. Beyond this, the book stated a program for social research which was already becoming much more acceptable to a large number of social scientists, who were just getting their breath back after the dramatic events of the first postwar decade—the sudden eruption of prosperity, the clash between the Soviet countries and the West, the appearance as vigorous independent nations of newly liberated colonial countries. From the early 1950s social criticism began to revive. Its new themes were the mass society, power, affluence, leisure, the problems and prospects of the third world; and only to a lesser extent the familiar problems of an earlier age of criticism, the outlook for capitalism as an economic system, or the relations between social classes.

One of the first and most influential works of the new criticism was David Riesman's *The Lonely Crowd* (1950). The title itself suggests the theme of "mass society"; the horde of private, unrelated, uncertain, leaderless individuals. The intention of the book was to show how changes in the American character, associated with changes in the social structure, had produced a mass society, and to criticize the quality of its life. In describing types of character, Riesman made use of three terms: tradition-directed, inner-directed, and other-directed. Broadly, these refer to the different ways in which men face the problems of their community life; they may deal with such problems either on the basis of customary rules, or by applying a standard which they have accepted as binding upon their own conduct (a moral imperative), or finally by seeking to conform with what the neighbors are doing, or at least what they think the neighbors are doing. Riesman's chief concern was with the change which he thought had taken place between the early nineteenth century, when Americans, he suggested, were largely inner-directed (by the Protestant ethic), and the mid-twentieth century, when they had become other-directed; that is, anxious to conform as closely as possible with the apparent values of those groups in which they found themselves. Two subsidiary themes of the book were the transition from a work-oriented to a consumption and leisure-oriented society; and the replacement of a ruling class, which might engender an opposition, by a collection of veto-groups to which everyone in some capacity belonged, and which substituted checks, balances and adjustments for the old clash of social and political interests and ideals. The declining importance of work as something which required effort, skill and judgment, and which brought the reward of an inner satisfaction, itself contributed to the decline of the Protestant ethic, which had emphasized the idea of work as a vocation, and had associated it in the American context with individual competence and ambition. Leisure does not call for the same dedication or seriousness, but rather for the qualities of being agreeable and tolerant. Moreover, in the past century the character of work itself has changed, and success in an occupation has also come to depend to a much greater extent upon being what is called a well-adjusted person. Similarly in political life, the inner-directed individual who "is related to the political scene either by his morality, his well-defined interests, or both," gives way to the other-directed individual who "leaves it to the group to defend his interests, co-operating when called upon to vote, to apply pressure, and so on."

The critical views of Mills and Riesman are alike in certain respects. Both see a tendency toward conformism and a curious collectivism of opinion in the American society of the early 1950s. Both attribute to the new middle classes an important influence in promoting this tendency. Finally, both see a possible way out through the efforts of the intellectuals. Mills exhorts the intellectuals to resume their critical attitude toward the established authorities and ideas; while Riesman concludes that "a vastly greater stream of creative, utopian thinking is needed" before any real progress can be made toward a more autonomous type of social character. Yet neither of them was entirely hopeful about the possible achievements of intellectual criticism. Mills observed often enough that the nineteenth century ideologies of liberalism and socialism—both products of the Enlightenment—were in ruins, and that nothing had yet appeared to take their place. Riesman viewed the mid-twentieth century as a time of disenchantment, when it was "easier to concentrate on programs for choosing between lesser evils" than to propose any new utopias.

In some other respects the ideas of Mills and Riesman diverge quite widely. Mills, although he did not accept Marxism as an adequate theory of society (and even less as a political creed), was still largely concerned with the problems of society and with the bases of political power in the terms which Marx had established. Riesman ignored most of this in order to concentrate upon a cultural transformation which had made leisure more important than work, consumption more important than production in

fashioning the nature of American society and its problems. The creative Utopian thought for which he called
was to be applied principally to discovering new kinds of
leisure activity in a society which already enjoyed material
abundance. The problem was seen as one of cultural innovation, rather than political change.

It should be evident that the critical ideas which I have
discussed so far do not amount to a new school of critical
thought. At times they converge upon the same problems,
at other times they are far apart. They are very different in
style, in method, and in their historical antecedents. For all
his scepticism about it Mills draws largely upon the Marxist tradition; Riesman draws upon Freud and the psycho-
analysts, and upon those anthropologists who have attempted to describe the cultural characteristics of whole
societies. There is little here which resembles the coherent
philosophical outlook of the pragmatists in the progressive
era, and it would be extraordinarily difficult to find any
close philosophical kinships among these and other critics
who were writing in the early 1950s.

Equally, it is difficult to trace any immediate influence
of their ideas. They appealed, as I have said, especially to
the intellectuals, but few listened to them at first. Most of
the intellectuals were on the defensive, where they were
not completely reconciled with their society. The editors
of *Partisan Review* published in 1952 a symposium on the
intellectuals in America in which they observed that:
"American intellectuals now regard America and its institutions in a new way. . . . For better or worse, most
writers no longer accept alienation as the artist's fate in
America; on the contrary, they want very much to be
part of American life." At this time, the ideas of Riesman
and especially of Mills found a much more responsive au-

dience in Europe than in North America. But how the situation has changed since then! For better or worse "alienation" has become one of the key words in the discourse of American intellectuals, and no one would now be tempted to describe their attitudes to society in the terms used by the editors of *Partisan Review* only a little more than a decade ago. There has been an intellectual revolt. It has drawn its sustenance from the ideas of a few social critics in America, from a much wider revolt against the tyranny of orthodox (or more precisely, official and state-imposed) Marxism, and from new movements of social protest. Its evolution reveals how close is the interdependence between social criticism as an intellectual phenomenon and the practical social movements which seek to change the working institutions of society.

CHAPTER 5

LEFT

AND

RIGHT

One of the things that prevented the formation of a more integrated body of social criticism in the 1950s was the defection of the philosophers. No thinker of the stature of Dewey came forward to present a general justification for the diverse lines of criticism, or to link them together in a comprehensive social philosophy. In any case, postwar philosophy in the Anglo-Saxon countries came to be dominated by the linguistic philosophers, who not only showed little interest in social and political doctrines, but held that the elaboration of such doctrines was no concern of a philosopher, and insinuated that there was something reprehensible in dealing with general ideas at all. Such views had a depressing effect in Britain, and I think also in North America; an effect which was in sharp contrast with the quickening influence of Marxism and existentialism in continental Europe during the same period. The editor of an English symposium on philosophy and politics felt able to announce solemnly, and with a certain satisfaction, that "For the moment, anyway, political philosophy is dead";[1] while an American, Daniel Bell, gave to his collection of essays on political themes the title *The End of Ideology: On the Exhaustion of Political Ideas in the Fifties.*

In North America, these philosophical attitudes, coinciding with the defensiveness of intellectuals under the pressures of McCarthyism, and the absence of any important left-wing social movements, produced an unadventurous, largely conformist state of mind. Writers like Mills and Riesman were at first voices crying in the wilderness, and as I suggested earlier, they were probably more appreciated in Europe than in America. Even in 1960 Mills could write, in a published letter to British Socialists: "When I settle down to write to you, I feel somehow 'freer' than usual. The reason, I suppose, is that most of the time I am writing for people whose ambiguities and values I imagine to be rather different from mine, but with you I feel enough in common to allow us to 'get on with it' in more positive ways."[2]

The one major philosophical thinker who, at this time,

---

[1] P. Laslett (editor), *Philosophy, Politics and Society* (1956), p. vii.

[2] C. Wright Mills, Letter to The New Left, *New Left Review*, (5), Sept.-Oct. 1960, p. 18.

undertook a re-examination of the whole condition of man in modern industrial society—Hannah Arendt—found herself in much the same situation as the sociological critics. Her books, *The Origins of Totalitarianism* (1951), *The Human Condition* (1958), and *On Revolution* (1963), are inspired by German existentialist philosophy, and they have probably made their chief impression upon European thinkers, rather than setting off a new movement of philosophical and social criticism in the United States. This is not to say that they lack any affinity with other critical writings. The theme which Miss Arendt expounds in *The Human Condition*—the dilemma of a society which has glorified labor, and which is about to be liberated from labor—is evidently connected with some of the ideas expressed by Riesman in *The Lonely Crowd,* and with the discussion of work and leisure, from a more strictly economic aspect, by J. K. Galbraith in *The Affluent Society.*

Miss Arendt is, however, the most pessimistic and the most conservative of these critics. "What we are confronted with," she writes, "is the prospect of a society of laborers without labor, that is, without the only activity left to them. Surely, nothing could be worse." The advent of mass leisure, the fulfillment of an age-old dream of freedom from labor, is seen as a problem because the society in which it is occurring no longer knows of "those other higher and more meaningful activities for the sake of which this freedom would deserve to be won," and there is "no aristocracy of either a political or spiritual nature from which a restoration of the other capacities of man could start anew."

Riesman's view is a more hopeful one. The great expansion of leisure demands new creative thinking in order to bestow upon leisure activities the kind of significance for the individual that work, occupying almost the whole of most men's time, once had. A social pattern has now to be created from leisure pursuits as it was formerly created out of economic activities. But Riesman does not see the problem as insoluble, nor does he consider that it could only be solved by an aristocracy, whether political or spiritual, which would establish new social values in an authoritative manner.

Galbraith is the most optimistic of all. He regards affluence as an undoubted blessing, and he is full of ideas as to how its benefits may be realized. He is mainly critical of what he calls the conventional economic wisdom, which is dazzled by the tremendous output of consumer goods and has not recognized their declining importance in an affluent society. With the growth of productivity, according to Galbraith, there appear a number of alternatives to the rapid and limitless increase in the output of consumer goods. One is the expansion of leisure time, either by reducing hours of work (as has happened steadily over the past century), or by reducing the numbers of people who work (as is now happening through the establishment of retirement plans, and especially through the extension of the period of education). Another is to devote resources to making work itself easier and more pleasant. A third is to develop as much as possible those occupations which are already found enjoyable, because they call for intelligence and skill and are based upon educational attainments. This is already coming about through the growth of scientific, managerial, and cultural activities, and Galbraith advocates the greatest possible expansion of the new class whose members are engaged in such activities. A final possibility, linked with the foregoing, is the diversion of resources from the private to the public sphere. The contrast between private opulence and public squalor is so great, in Galbraith's view, that a considerable part of the resources made available by increasing productivity ought now to be devoted to restoring public amenities both in the towns and in the countryside.

The ideas of Riesman and Galbraith, unlike those of Hannah Arendt, belong to a tradition of liberal and progressive thought, but they are a good deal less radical than those of Wright Mills; and they seem to me to neglect, at least in the books I have been discussing, two important questions. The first is that of political power. Galbraith, in particular, seems to assume that the social changes which he regards as desirable will come about automatically, merely as a result of increasing prosperity and the gradual abandonment of conventional ideas. But this appears very doubtful. The transfer of resources from private consumption to public works, for example, raises political questions —of taxation, of the scope of government action, and of the balance between military and civil expenditure—which can only be decided through a confrontation of interests and doctrines. Or to take another instance: it may be very desirable to use some of our wealth to make work easier and more pleasant, but Galbraith does not give any precise indication as to how this is to be effected. One might suppose from his account that American industry was a socially directed process, instead of being, as it is, a collection of privately owned enterprises. Who is to say that the owners and controllers of industry will in fact decide that one desirable employment of their increasing output is to add to the enjoyment of the work itself? Again this seems to me a political question, which would involve major decisions about the degree of public control of economic life, and even the working out of a comprehensive economic philosophy.

A second question which is somewhat inadequately treated by these critics is that of equality. In the one brief chapter of *The Affluent Society* which is devoted to this subject Galbraith observes that there has been "a decline of interest in inequality as an economic issue," that it has ceased to preoccupy men's minds, and that the progressive increase of aggregate output is now seen as an alternative to redistribution. I think that this view is to some extent an illusion produced by the temporary conditions of sudden and unaccustomed prosperity. Rising aggregate output has resulted, in most of the industrial countries, in lessening the harsh contrasts between rich and poor; but it has by no means done away with the differences, or with the strong sentiments they arouse, either in the United States or elsewhere. One of the discoveries of recent years has been the extent of poverty in supposedly affluent societies, a discovery made not only by social scientists, but by the poor themselves; in the United States, for example, by the large Negro population. It would scarcely be necessary to have a war against poverty if the problem were not serious, or if its solution could safely be left to the automatic growth of aggregate output.

There is another aspect of this question which raises some doubts in my mind. When Galbraith proposes a transfer of resources from private consumption to public services, and the use of our growing resources to increase the numbers of non-workers, whether these are the young who are to be educated for a longer period, or the old who are to retire earlier and with higher incomes, he does not seem to recognize fully that such measures may involve a substantial redistribution of income, and thus depend in this way too upon political decisions. The more I reflect upon the notion of a society in which there will be mass leisure, the more I am persuaded that it involves a much greater degree of economic equality than any present day society has begun to approach. For if leisure is to be the principal element in the social life of the near future then there will have to be provided, on a much more equal basis, the means to use it and enjoy it. It is the lack of resources to make full use of leisure time, among a large part of the population, that already presents us with some grave social problems.

The means indicated for achieving this society of abundance and leisure also point toward a greater economic equality, since they involve the extension of automation and the education of a large part of the population to a much higher level. In a society in which most work would consist in the technical supervision of machines, in administrative, professional, and cultural activities, and in the scientific planning and regulation of the economy as a whole, there would not be the same case for, nor the possibility of, such great income differentiation as has existed in conditions where the highly educated form a small minority, and where the cultural differences between them and the unskilled and semi-skilled manual workers are profound.

I should like to make one last comment upon the ideas of Riesman and Galbraith with regard to equality. Outside the problems of economic equality which I have mentioned they seem to me to take altogether too little account of those political inequalities with which C. Wright Mills was so much concerned. I agree with them that we need to think imaginatively about the emerging society of abundance and leisure, and especially about the cultural changes and the new institutions which mass leisure will require. I share their qualified optimism, as against Hannah Arendt's rather pessimistic outlook. But I do not think that we can simply put aside as relatively unimportant the economic and political arrangements of our society. Abundance and leisure will, in my view, call for changes in economic and political institutions just as profound as those in the organization of leisure. Indeed, it may be just the economic and political changes—an approach toward solving the problem of inequalities of power and responsibility—which will make possible the advent of this brave new world.

At all events it is plain to see that disagreements over the distribution of economic resources and political power still divide the left from the right in politics, and that in the 1960s they have had a revival with the emergence of a New Left, and on a smaller scale a New Right in the United States. It is fairly easy to date the beginnings of the New Left as an international phenomenon. The crucial year was 1956. That was the year when British and French imperialism had their final, anachronistic and unsuccessful fling at Suez, when the Hungarian intellectuals and workers revolted against Stalinism, when in Poland some of the institutions of the Stalinist system were more quietly dismantled. The Suez affair produced in Britain the most extensive revolt of the intellectuals since the 1930s, while the events in Hungary and Poland led many to give up their allegiance to the Communist Party. These two movements together gave rise to the New Left, which found a practical expression in such movements as the Campaign for Nuclear Disarmament and an intellectual expression in the *New Left Review*. In France, it was not so much the Suez incident as the Hungarian revolution, the war in Algeria and the decay of Stalinism which created the New Left. In the United States it was likewise the events in eastern Europe, and in addition the Cuban revolution, the course of American foreign policy in Latin America and in southeast Asia, and the Negro revolt, which together inspired a revival of the Left. These diverse influences are apparent in the various movements which have emerged in the U.S.A.—the Student Nonviolent Coordinating Committee (S.N.C.C.), the Students for a Democratic Society (S.D.S.), the W.E.B. DuBois Clubs, The Free Speech Movement at Berkeley, the Vietnam Day Committees—and in the new journals of the 1960s: *Studies on the Left, Liberation, Ramparts* and others.

What is new about this New Left? First of all, it is less dogmatic in outlook and less exclusively political in its commitment than was the Left in the 1930s. Radical critics today have not accepted any existing social system as an ideal to which they can give their undeviating allegiance with anything like the fervor which some intellectuals of the 1930s displayed in their attachment to the U.S.S.R. At the most, the radical intellectuals have committed themselves to the support of the developing countries in the "third world" and of the revolutionary movements which have appeared there. The avoidance of dogmatism, and in a more extreme form the outright rejection of any ideology, is in some measure a consequence of the lack of any comprehensive and convincing social theory, and of the widespread uncertainty about social ideals. But it also reflects some more positive attitudes—humanism allied with scepticism, or at least with an experimental and empirical approach to problems; an egalitarianism which repudiates the exposition of some orthodox doctrine by infallible teachers; and a strong belief in the importance of personal moral choices. The divergent interpretations of the promise and dangers of affluence and mass leisure, the demonstration of the problems which industrialization and

mechanization bring in their wake in every society, whatever the regime under which it lives, have brought into
question the uncomplicated faith of earlier generations of
radicals and socialists. Hence the concern of the New Left
with a great variety of issues outside the economic and
political spheres; with education and cultural life, and
with social relations in the everyday affairs of the neigh-
borhood or work place. Hence, also, the influence on the
international scene of such American critics as Mills, Riesman and Galbraith, who have already had to confront,
each in his own style, the phenomena of affluence, the mass
society, and anomie which are now appearing in the European countries.

The attitudes of the New Left toward Marxism—and
especially toward the ideas of Marx himself—are revealing.
It is a different aspect of Marx's thought, the sociological
and philosophical rather than the economic, which now
attracts most attention; and it is discussed in a far more
scholarly fashion than was ever the case in the 1930s. The
Marxian theme which has figured most prominently in
recent debates is that of "alienation"; the notion that in
certain forms of society man becomes separated from the
products of his own labor, and that this separation is the
prime source of misery, conflict and revolt. This idea has
provided a starting point for criticism along different
lines; criticism of capitalist society in which man is separated from his material products as a result of the private
ownership of industry; of collectivist society in which a
similar separation proceeds from the centralized political
and bureaucratic control of production; of mass society in
which man loses his control over political decisions; and of
technological society in which he finds his life regulated by
the very machines whose creator he is. If the lines of criti-

cism are diverse, so too are the conclusions reached and the solutions proposed. Some of the more conventional Marxists would regard class divisions as the source of all alienation, and they seem to anticipate with an almost religious exaltation the "end of alienation" in a classless society. More common, however, and in my view more fruitful, is a sociological approach which seeks to discover the extent to which men have lost the power to direct their own lives in different types of modern society, and which goes on to consider the practical ways in which they could take a more active part in deciding how their material and intellectual creations are to be used, and how the pattern of their social life is to be arranged without subordinating the individual entirely to the group and without producing a mediocre uniformity. Both Mills and Riesman were concerned with some aspects of alienation in this sense; and the social movements of the New Left have been involved with such problems in practical and experimental ways, in the university, in poverty programs and in the civil rights campaigns. But it is evident that there is no theory which is accepted as explaining it all, no doctrine which provides a sure guide through the variety of situations which have to be confronted. No orthodoxy prevails, and few participants in the New Left suppose that the clue to understanding is to be had from Marx alone.

The present radicalism has developed from the series of events, domestic and foreign, of the 1950s which I described earlier, and it is still the diversified expression of a variety of social movements, particularly in the United States, rather than a meeting ground for those who accept a distinctive social theory. Many of those who take part in the social movements—civil rights, the student movement, community projects, the peace movement—would perhaps not even understand exactly the sense of "belonging to the Left," and some might deny that the traditional distinction between Left and Right was any longer significant. They would attribute a greater importance to the difference between generations, and this is an aspect of the new radicalism which I shall examine more closely in a later chapter.

C. Wright Mills, who was one of the leading intellectual representatives of the New Left, himself had no comprehensive social theory to expound, and he offered a redefinition of Left and Right which cuts across the older meaning of these terms. According to Mills, the Right means "celebrating society as it is," the Left means criticizing society and producing political demands and programs. In an older terminology this would have been said differently: that the Right means "celebrating *capitalist* society as it is," while the Left means "criticizing capitalist society and producing programs for a *socialist* society." The reasons for the change in language are not difficult to discover. One is the appearance of new conditions, some of which I have mentioned briefly: affluence and expanding leisure, the stark contrast between rich and poor nations in the modern world which often overshadows the differences between rich and poor within the advanced industrial countries. Another reason, perhaps more important, is the historical development of socialism, especially in the U.S.S.R., during this century. If capitalism could be criticized for having failed to achieve the liberty and justice which were proclaimed by the French Revolution, then socialism, in its Russian form, could be criticized for a still more blatant failure to achieve them, or even for restoring their opposites. In short, social criticism, which had meant in the latter part of the nineteenth century and up to the 1930s principally a left-wing criticism of capitalist society, must now be taken to embrace the critical examination of both capitalism and socialism, and of some conditions—bureaucracy, for example—which are to be found in both types of society. Criticism and vindication can no longer be so easily assigned to the traditional categories of Left and Right.

Mills and other American critics have certainly taken this view. For my part, I am not persuaded that the older conceptions of Left and Right should be quite so completely abandoned—although they clearly need to be revised—in favor of the new distinction between social criticism and celebration of the *status quo*. There are several important ideas—on one side those of equality and participation, on the other those of leadership and authority—which still mark a profound difference between the Left and the Right. In the movements of social protest in the United States these ideas have a significant influence, which I shall consider in the next chapter, despite the fact that they have not been brought together in a distinctive new ideology.

Some of the differences between Left and Right are evident also from an examination of recent social movements and ideas of the Right in the United States. The right-wing movements which have attracted most attention, those which have been called the extreme or radical right, are in the main a continuation of McCarthyism, although they can also be connected with earlier movements. They present a problem of sociological rather than intellectual interest. More important in the present context is the revival, or perhaps one should say the beginnings, of a conservative political philosophy in the United States. This phenomenon deserves attention, if only because of the extreme difficulty of the enterprise. In saying this I do not mean to suggest that it is difficult to *be* a conservative, in the sense of wanting to maintain for oneself or one's social group the *status quo* of the moment, or in the sense which Riesman gives to it when he speaks of being "quite conservative" because he wants to conserve America as a going concern (though this is an ambiguous phrase). What I mean is that it is difficult in America to establish the philosophical ground of conservatism. In Europe, and especially in Britain, a conservative doctrine could be formulated in the manner of Burke, or of a modern descendant such as Michael Oakeshott, as the view that men should follow so far as possible those institutions and customs of their society which have existed time out of mind, and which embody the wisdom of many generations; that they should be guided by a long-established tradition of political behavior and not by abstract, rationalistic recipes for a good society. But such a political philosophy is hardly possible in America. In the first place the society's institutions have not existed since time immemorial, but were rather suddenly created a little less than two centuries ago (just about the time in fact when Burke was deploring such revolutionary changes). And secondly, the resulting tradition is itself liberal and progressive. As one observer of the United States has put it admirably: "America is . . . conservative in fundamental principles . . . But the principles conserved are liberal, and some, indeed, are radical."[8]

Conservative philosophers in America, therefore, have in a sense to invent a traditional conservative society, or else to call for radical measures to establish one. Thus they become social critics, not simply the defenders of an existing order. There is a good recent example in a work by E.

[8] Gunnar Myrdal, *An American Dilemma*, p. 7.

Digby Baltzell, *The Protestant Establishment* (1964), which criticizes at length the development of modern American society, and urges the re-creation (though I would see it as the creation) of an upper-class establishment which would produce and perpetuate "a set of traditional standards which carry authority and to which the rest of society aspires." This kind of instant tradition may be possible, but I doubt it. You have either to be traditional or to be new and modern, and the United States is overwhelmingly the latter.

This account may indicate both the relevance of the distinction between Left and Right, since there are to be found expositions of opposed political philosophies, even though they draw heavily upon European traditions; and also the extent to which in the United States this distinction is obscured or overlaid. Thinkers of the Left and of the Right may both become social critics and even radicals —though usually in different styles. Their criticisms may sometimes converge upon the same issues: the criticisms of the other-directed society by Riesman, and of the mass society by Mills, have some affinities with the ideas of more conservative thinkers. Since the 1930s, moreover, the radicals of the Left have had to look more critically not only at the doctrines of socialism but at its practice in the socialist countries, and the conclusions at which they have arrived are diverse and often tentative. These considerations help to explain the present confusion of social criticism, the inclination of many critics to present their ideas as extremely personal judgments upon the state of society, the resistance of many participants in the social movements to any attempts to connect their activities with a theory of society or a political doctrine, and the lack of agreement or even clarity about what is being attacked in present-day society and what is to replace it. For some active radicals the social movements appear to have become themselves an alternative form of society; and these critics might well reiterate Bernstein's saying (without its qualifications) that "the ultimate aim . . . is nothing, the movement is everything."

CHAPTER 6

THE

SOCIAL

MOVEMENTS

The audience of the critics whose writings I have discussed has grown considerably since the mid-1950s. One sign of this is the appearance of popular expositions of their ideas. Consider a book such as William H. Whyte's *The Organization Man,* which received much acclaim when it was published in 1956. Entertainingly written, it sets out in a more popular style ideas on mass society and conformism similar to those of Riesman in *The Lonely Crowd.* Whyte contrasts the Protestant ethic of an earlier

America with what he calls the "social ethic" of modern America. The former stressed the values of individualism, hard work, thrift, and competition; the latter stresses the importance of the group and of "belongingness." The principal bearer of this new ethic is the business executive; and the group to which he feels a need to belong, to which he is urged to be "loyal," is the business corporation. Whyte portrays him in different contexts; in the organization itself where batteries of personality tests are employed to select and advance the well-rounded, conforming man, and in the suburb, where he (and still more his wife) is prone to sacrifice individual tastes for the sake of fitting into the community. An examination of popular fiction and films, Whyte suggests, shows the same drift towards conformity; it is no longer the rugged individualist, answerable to his own conscience, who is presented as the hero, but the man who follows undeviatingly the rules and customs of his group.

These and other themes of criticism appear likewise in the writings of Vance Packard. The very titles show the influence of the sociological critics. *The Hidden Persuaders* deals with the power of advertisers and the mass media, *The Status Seekers* with conformism and "belongingness," *The Waste Makers* with conspicuous consumption and the drive to an unlimited increase of production regardless of its social value, *The Pyramid Climbers* with the urge to economic success and social mobility—which is more and more often presented in the unattractive guise of the rat race.

One feature of this popular criticism which deserves attention is that it is addressed largely to the new middle classes, who are also presumably its most devoted readers. Its style is satirical. It holds up to the middle classes a slightly distorting mirror in which their virtues as well as their vices take on a ridiculous aspect. It is successful, as other forms of satire have been in the past decade, because it responds to an existing uneasiness about whether prosperity and an assured place on the social escalator do in fact amount to a good life. The same malaise which Wright Mills sketched in *White Collar* is reflected in this criticism.

At the same time such popular criticism is very much restricted to the middle-class milieu. The social scientist who reads *The Organization Man* is likely to be struck especially by the tameness and unimaginativeness of its conclusions. These amount to little more than the true but trite observations that there is always some tension and possibility of opposition between the individual and society; and that in an age when the claims of large organizations are pressed so strongly it may be more important to emphasize the values of individualism than those of cooperation with the group. This leaves unanswered a great number of questions. Is there no difference between the kinds of loyalty which may be expected toward different organizations; between loyalty to a nation, a class, a church, an academic community, or a business concern? Is there no difference between organizations in the degree of conformity which they expect or exact? Is not one of the major problems revealed by *The Organization Man* simply that a particular kind of organization, the business firm, which should be merely an instrument, has set itself up in the United States as a way of life and a source of ultimate values?

Another problem which stands out from the pages of *The Organization Man* is the ambiguity of the "social ethic." This ethic expresses a desire for community, but the community which it proposes is extraordinarily narrow and uninspiring; it is that of one's local peer group, or at most the members of one's own social stratum. As Whyte observes, although the social ethic has a collectivist tinge about it, the ideal society which it vaguely suggests is not socialism, but feudalism, with its clearly delineated ranks, its corporations, and its closely integrated village or manorial life. In the new society guided by the social ethic the business firm is to become a modern version of the medieval guild, the suburb a modern village, in which everyone knows his place and feels that he belongs. Evidently, the "social ethic" might be more broadly interpreted as a concern with bringing into a national community, and into its constituent local communities, those groups of people who are in practice excluded from it; for instance, ethnic minorities and the poor. So conceived it would be an incitement to a more searching criticism of American society and culture. Whyte makes plain that this is not how it works in fact; it does not broaden men's understanding of the larger society, nor does it increase their curiosity or concern about the conditions of life of men outside their own circle. On the contrary it confines them more rigorously in the narcissistic contemplation of their own small worlds.

Yet Whyte himself does not examine at any length these potentially conflicting versions of the social ethic, and on one occasion at least, he confuses them. He refers to Erich Fromm's book, *The Sane Society*, which deals with group conformity as an escape from the burdens of freedom, and which takes as one example of such conformity the suburban life of Park Forest, Chicago, where Whyte had conducted some of his own inquiries. As a solution of the problem of conformism Erich Fromm advocates "democratic communitarianism," but Whyte argues that this is not a real solution because it would only reproduce the kind of group pressure upon the individual which is already found in suburbs such as Park Forest. This is to miss the main point of Fromm's discussion. His psychological analysis of modern capitalist society treats conformity as only one element in a more complex situation; in his own words, ". . . man regresses to a receptive and marketing orientation and ceases to be productive; . . . he loses his sense of self, becomes dependent on approval, hence tends to conform and yet to feel insecure; he is dissatisfied, bored and anxious. . . ."[1] The analysis is followed by proposals for a "sane society" in which there would be justice as well as "belongingness," individual freedom and responsibility as well as community; and Fromm makes quite plain that in order to attain such a social order there would need to be far-reaching changes in the economic, the political and the cultural arrangements of American society. These changes are set out in some detail: in the economic sphere, from a system of private ownership and control of production to one of workers' self-management, and from an exclusive concern with increasing output as such to the planning of socially desirable production, which would include the renewal of public amenities and massive aid to the poverty-stricken countries; in the political sphere, from a mode of life which treats politics as an exceptional and sporadic activity, so far as the mass of the people are concerned, to one which encourages a more sustained interest and participation in both local and national

---

[1] Erich Fromm: *The Sane Society*, p. 270. The cult which has developed in recent years around the so-called mind-expanding drugs provides another illustration of Fromm's ideas on the progressive deterioration of a sense of self. The literature of the cult reveals, even more than a despairing rebelliousness, a desperate quest for some means of regaining this lost sense of self. We should now perhaps reverse Marx's dictum and say that "opium is the religion of the people."

politics; in the cultural sphere, a change above all in education, from the narrow preoccupation with training young people for highly specialized careers to a conception of education as the awakening and sustenance of critical thought and as the basis for creating a distinctive civilization.

The popular writers have simplified, occasionally distorted, and diffused more widely the ideas of such social critics as Mills, Riesman and Fromm. For the most part, also, they have concentrated upon the issues which affect the new suburban middle classes, and they have been inclined to ignore those problems in the United States which are most explosive in character and which have provoked the recent activities of radical political movements. It is in this sphere, however, that some of the most important critical ideas of the 1960s have found their expression and have had their real influence. In general, it is the case that the most vigorous social criticism is to be found during periods of rapid social change when movements of political protest also flourish. The most obvious and extensive example in modern times is the development of Marxism and of other socialist doctrines during the latter half of the nineteenth century, in a close relationship with the rise of the European labor movement. In North America, the populist and socialist doctrines of the 1880s coincided with the closing of the frontier, the first appearance of gross economic inequalities, and the agrarian protest movements; the era of the progressive thinkers in the first decade of this century coincided with the growth of an industrial working class and of militant trade unions; and the left-wing social doctrines of the 1930s were responses to the world economic crisis and to the political conflicts which erupted within and between nations.

In the same way, the social criticism of the 1960s—

although some of its intellectual antecedents are to be found in the writings of social critics during the previous decade—is particularly associated with movements of social protest: with the Negro revolt, the student movement, and the peace movement. In any such association there is a two-way intellectual traffic between criticism and protest. The social movements produce new ideas about their problems and about possible solutions, while the critics seek to interpret on a broader scale the meaning of the social conflicts in which the movements are involved. It is with this intellectual aspect—with ideas and criticism—that I shall be concerned in the present context, not with the organization or achievements of the protest movements as such.[2]

Let us consider first the Negro revolt and the civil rights movement. In a sense these are nothing new: Negro movements for civil and political rights have been going on since before the Civil War, and as Negro leaders say, they have been asking the white Americans for more than a century now to get off their backs. The continuity of this struggle during the present century is exemplified by the career of W.E.B. Du Bois, a founder of the National Association for the Advancement of Colored People in 1909, a sponsor of the Negro literary and artistic renaissance of the 1920s, a supporter of the U.S.S.R. and an editor of *New Masses* in the 1930s, and an active opponent of Cold War policies in the immediate postwar years. What *is* new is the extent and vigor of the revolt. Beginning with the "sit-in" demonstrations of 1960 and the formation of S.N.C.C. in the same year, the movement has developed on a massive scale through marches, rallies and riots.[3] Many factors

[2] There is a good survey of the movements and a useful selection of documents in Paul Jacobs and Saul Landau, *The New Radicals* (1966).

[3] For a brief account see C. Vann Woodward, *The Strange Career of Jim Crow* (2nd ed. 1965) Chapter V. See also the valuable collection

have contributed to this Negro awakening, but most observers would agree that one major influence has been the example of the independent African states. When all Negroes were under some kind of foreign rule or tutelage there was no real model of independence to which American Negroes could look, nor was there a sufficiently widespread confidence in their ability to become self-directing. With the rise of the new African nations, and with the growth of their influence in world politics, a different prospect appeared. For some Negroes, such as Malcolm X and the Black Nationalists, the conflict in the United States came to appear as a national independence struggle, and they advocated the formation of a separate Negro state. For the great majority of Negroes, however, the primary aim of their struggle is to secure full acceptance in present-day American society. There are resemblances here to the early labor movement in Europe, with its demands for the right to vote, for greater economic equality, for security of employment, and for access to education. Where the Negro revolt differs from the labor movement is in not proposing radical changes in the society itself in order to achieve these ends. Most Negroes, and most of their leaders, still see as the great fault of American society that it does not admit them to its benefits; that the Negro is worse paid, worse educated, worse housed than white Americans.

Nevertheless, there are Negro critics who envisage something more than a greater equality between white and black in an otherwise unchanged social system. James Baldwin, for example, has written: "How can one respect, let alone adopt, the values of a people who do not, on any

of documents in Alan F. Westin (editor), *Freedom Now! The Civil Rights Struggle in America* (1964).

level whatever, live the way they say they do, or the way they say they should? I cannot accept the proposition that the four-hundred-year travail of the American Negro should result merely in his attainment of the present level of the American civilization. I am far from convinced that being released from the African witch doctor was worthwhile if I am now—in order to support the moral contradictions and the spiritual aridity of my life—expected to become dependent upon the American psychiatrist. It is a bargain I refuse. The only thing white people have that black people need, or should want, is power—and no one holds power forever."[4]

It has still to be seen what effect the civil rights movement will have upon the outlook of the Negro people as a whole; whether it will engender a new social philosophy and contribute to the revival of a progressive movement, or whether it will result only in a modest improvement of living conditions for the poorest strata and greater ease in the assimilation of middle-class Negroes. At the present time only a small minority of those who are involved in the Negro revolt seem to connect it with any more comprehensive reconstruction of society. The community programs which S.N.C.C. developed in some areas of the south have served as models for the poverty programs elsewhere, and they have inspired some of the discussions of "democratic participation" as a basic principle which ought to be applied throughout social life; but relatively few people have yet been touched by such ideas.

Not surprisingly, radical ideas have been most intensely discussed in the student movement, and since the student organizations have been active in civil rights, in the war on poverty, and in the peace movement, their ideas have been

---

[4] James Baldwin, *The Fire Next Time*, p. 110.

widely diffused. Here I propose to examine primarily those aspects of the student movement which are concerned more strictly with the university itself and with the American system of education. The revolt at Berkeley in the fall of 1964 has brought notoriety to the movement. It began with student grievances concerning freedom of speech on the campus, but it soon came to embrace much larger issues—the nature of the modern university and its relations with society, as well as the place of students within the university—and it has now spread widely to other universities in the United States, in Canada, and even in Europe.

The idea of a university which the students opposed and attacked was that of the "knowledge factory," in which students are processed as efficiently as possible for careers in the established social order outside. They contrasted this, however vaguely, with an older view of the university as a place in which knowledge may be pursued also for its own sake, or in the words of Irving Howe, as "a center for disinterested learning . . . quick with the passions of controversy yet dedicated to those studies which the outer world may dismiss as esoteric . . . a sanctuary for opinion," as "a place where it is possible to encounter men who will serve as models of intellectual discipline and enthusiasm."[5] Or again, as Lewis Mumford has written: ". . . the university might be called an active cloister; its function is the critical reappraisal and renewal of the cultural heritage."[6]

This is not how their university appeared to the students at Berkeley, or later on, to other students on other

[5] Irving Howe: Introduction to Michael V. Miller and Susan Gilmore (editors), *Revolution at Berkeley*, p. xii.
[6] Quoted by Howe, op. cit. p. xiii.

campuses. It was, in their eyes, a bureaucratically organized institution, thoroughly permeated by the values of the business corporation and the power elite. No one has argued that the university should be entirely remote from the life of society outside; sealed off, like some hothouse of the intellect, from its environment. But the students, and in the end many of the faculty, did argue that the values of the university should be clearly distinguished from those of the business and political worlds, and that if there was to be a traffic of ideas and opinions between these worlds, then the university should be able to stand forth as an autonomous body and an equal participant in any dialogue. Some, of course, would go further than this, and would give a pre-eminence to the university as a kind of cloister, to be cherished especially in a world which is increasingly ruled by commercial and military values.

The student movement, whatever its immediate success or lack of success, has brought into the public arena a number of important and as yet unresolved questions about higher education in the modern industrial, democratic societies. First, what is the purpose of a university in conditions in which a much larger proportion of the population may expect to enjoy a university education, and in which the effective working of society depends upon a highly educated populace? Many of the arguments for expanding higher education have concentrated upon the economic benefits which are likely to result; rising national output, and a higher lifetime income for graduates. This is the main case which is made, for instance, in the Robbins Report on the expansion of British universities. But no one has suggested that this is the sole justification for expansion; or, to take one example, that subjects such as philosophy, which have no conceivable relation to economic growth, ought to be abandoned. The thinkers of the eighteenth century enlightenment, and their nineteenth century successors, who advocated a massive development of education at all levels, saw it as an agency of civilization. Through education, men would become more rational, more self-directing, more reasonable and humane, and they would get more enjoyment from life.

This is still an ideal of the university but it is often endangered by suggestions that the university should simply respond to the demands of powerful agencies, economic and political, in the society outside. In some countries the principal danger arises from political interference; in the United States, although political pressures since the McCarthy period have succeeded in muting social criticism, a more insidious challenge to the independence of the university comes from the influence of the business world. There is no other country, I think, in which universities are so frequently (and so improperly) judged in terms of their standing with the "business community." This is understandable, since America is a business civilization; but it is not consistent with those older ideals of the university as a community devoted to learning and critical thought. Many university teachers themselves have been insufficiently zealous in defending the independence of the university and in resisting encroachments upon its liberties.[7] In the event, it was left for the students to speak out on their behalf.

The second matter raised with great urgency by the student movement is that of university organization and government. Here also the students have returned to an older view. A university is, or should be, a community of scholars. As such a community it ought to be largely self-

[7] One honorable exception is Jacques Barzun, whose book *The House of Intellect* is a splendid assertion of the claims of intellectual life and a condemnation of divers attempts to subvert it.

regulating; not governed from the outside by politicians, officials, or businessmen. Most of those who advance this view do not overlook that universities have always been subject to pressure, and to attempts at control, by external powers. The medieval universities, which are sometimes referred to as models of academic autonomy, had to contend with the powerful influence of princes and churchmen. In part because of such external constraints universities have very often failed to be the centers of creative and critical thought. Many of the founders of modern natural science worked outside the universities; the Encyclopaedists in France, the Utilitarians in England, were for the most part independent scholars; the founding fathers of sociology did not teach in universities; and the systematic study of the social sciences in the nineteenth century began in many cases in private colleges outside the established system of university education—in France, for example, in the *Ecole libre des sciences politiques;* and in England, in the *London School of Economics and Political Science.* What is surprising to recent critics in the student movement is that modern democracy does not seem as yet to have affected the government of universities. Why is it, indeed, that in many universities so few members of the governing bodies are directly elected by the academic community itself? There is perhaps a case to be made for the representation of outside interests in the councils of a university, because the university both serves and depends upon the surrounding community; but if this is accepted it should at least be clear that such representatives have mainly an advisory function and that they are supposed to reflect all the diverse interests of the community, including those of minorities and of dissenting groups. There is a larger aspect of this question to be considered. Among the reasons for advocating democratic self-government for the universities are, first, that this would extend the practical experience of exercising democratic rights (and it is essential that students as well as faculty should participate); and second, that it would establish more securely the independence of the intellectual community and thus be of direct benefit to the working of democratic institutions, if we accept the view that one vital element of democracy is the wide diffusion of power and influence among many different groups.

Not all of these ideas have been formulated clearly and precisely within the student movement, but they are implied, I think, by the importance which is attached to the general notion of "participatory democracy"; to a conception of democracy, that is, which requires the full participation of all those affected by significant policy decisions, in every sphere of life, in determining the nature of the decisions. The activities of students in the various social movements have helped to ensure a wide dissemination of ideas and the formation of a common language in which the aspirations of the movements are expressed. So far the most persuasive of the new ideas has been that of "participatory democracy." It challenges most directly the bureaucratic and impersonal administration of large organizations, from the business corporation to the "multiversity"; but in a more general way it is proposed as a solution of the problem of alienation, of man's loss of control over the ordering of his life. Early in this century Max Weber sketched a gloomy picture of the bureaucratic system that was becoming established in the leading industrial countries; a system in which every man would be a mere cog in the machine and with no other ambition than to become a slightly larger cog. The students at Berkeley, and in other social movements, thought that they had discovered an alternative. As one of them wrote about his experiences:

". . . the students achieved some unique results. They took the first genuine steps toward that sense of community everybody was always vainly searching for."

The third major social movement—the peace movement —has been largely preoccupied with the role of the United States in world affairs, but it has paid attention also to the repercussions of American foreign policy upon the domestic institutions of the society. Its overriding concern is with the division in the world between the western and communist countries, and with the part which the U.S.A. has played in the Cold War confrontation. The critics have posed some fundamental questions about the present American policies: first, whether it is the duty or the interest of the United States to oppose communism by force in every part of the world; secondly, whether it is always communism that is being opposed; thirdly, whether the time has not come for a more profound reappraisal of foreign policies in the light of the changes which have occurred in the European communist countries and in the international communist movement. The main focus of these criticisms is the war in Vietnam, where the United States is conducting, at immense cost, a military campaign on behalf of a manifestly unpopular regime against a government which is regarded by most Asian peoples (and by many outside Asia) as the leader of a national liberation movement. But the war in Vietnam is only one in a series of American actions which include the attempted intervention in Cuba, the successful intervention in the Dominican Republic, and the ill-fated Project Camelot;[8] and

[8] A project sponsored by the military authorities for studies of potentially revolutionary areas of the world, mainly in Latin America, with a view to developing effective counter-insurgency strategies. See the account by Irving L. Horowitz, "The Life and Death of Project Camelot" in *Transaction*, Vol. 3, No. 1, November–December, 1965.

which seem to the critics in the peace movement to establish the United States as the leader of counter-revolution in a world which is in the full flood of revolutionary social change.

A second theme of criticism associated with the foregoing deals with the re-birth of imperialism; a subject examined recently by Mr. Conor Cruise O'Brien in an essay on "Contemporary Forms of Imperialism."[9] Two questions are posed by the critics. Do the western nations, and the United States in particular, seek to dominate or control the developing nations through the use of economic power in place of the direct rule which they once exercised? And secondly, whether this is the case or not, do the developing countries in Africa, Asia and Latin America still see the western nations as imperialist powers? The critics would answer "yes" to both questions. The Suez adventure, the foreign interventions by American forces, the need to defend the widespread economic interests of the western nations, all suggest that the spirit of the nineteenth century imperialism is far from dead. Along with these old attitudes there still flourishes the notion of white supremacy, within the United States itself, and in its most brutal form in South Africa. In spite of international aid and the work of international agencies we are still very far from living in a world in which there is equality among peoples and races.

Lastly, the critics in the peace movement are concerned with the effects of military confrontation upon the structure and culture of their own society. The problems which they raise here are close to those discussed by C. Wright Mills in *The Power Elite*. Has the political and military struggle in the world led to an awful concentration of

[9] *Studies on the Left*, V (4), 1965, pp. 13–26.

power in the hands of a small group of political leaders, executives of the big corporations engaged in war production, and military chiefs? Has this elite, moreover, succumbed to a military view of world problems, to the fascination of its own "war games," to a dangerous belief in overwhelming victory and total success—a belief more appropriate to an earlier age not threatened with annihilation? Some of the consequences of the United States' involvement in the war in Vietnam are evident: the curtailment of programs to alleviate poverty, to improve schools, to extend needed social services. Other, more diffuse, less easily measurable consequences are suggested by the critics: a rising tide of unreason in political life, an intrusion of the "military-industrial complex" into many spheres of social life, including the university, where it subverts democracy, independence, the freedom to dissent, and cultural diversity. War and war-preparedness, in other words, are hastening the advent of the mass society.

The social movements have not only produced their own style of criticism; they have also provided an audience for the academic critics, a testing ground for their ideas, and a necessary link between social thought and action. Only since the movements developed on a large scale has there been serious discussion of whether a new radicalism, or a "New Left," is emerging in the United States. This question is still unanswered, not in the main because the radical movements still affect only a small minority of the population, but because the ideas which they express are so diverse and apparently unrelated. It is easy enough to distinguish some major themes of criticism, and even to divine a certain community of ideas, as I have already suggested. The critics deal with the threat of nuclear war, with the excessive concentration of power in overwhelmingly large organizations, with social inequality, with the spread of bureaucracy and the dehumanization of life, with the deterioration of taste and the decline of individuality. But they respond to the present state of American society with a variety of ideas and in diverse styles. A few choose exile, as in the 1920s. Some use satire, a form of criticism practised by the impotent who know that they are impotent. They are the court jesters of the modern establishment. Most of the critics enter the opposition, either joining a movement or withdrawing from society, on the basis of a private moral judgment, while carefully avoiding anything which appears to them as a political orthodoxy. The most widely held philosophical view among the New Left is probably some version of existentialism, precisely because this emphasizes personal choice and decision, the direct human response to a situation, in a world which appears increasingly impersonal.

Yet I doubt if such a creed is adequate to sustain effective social criticism or to bring about any radical social change. Left-wing critics such as Sartre have had to supplement the individualistic and moral stance of existentialism with the historical and sociological ideas of Marxism in their effort to create a more satisfactory guide to social action. Above all, they have had to outline, in however sketchy a manner, some alternative conception of society— for which they have often turned to the revolutionary nations of the third world—in order to give point to their criticism and protest. It is very well to repulse those smelly little orthodoxies which put the mind in chains again (yet we should remember that Orwell was speaking of the doctrines of narrow and intolerant political sects in the 1930s, not of the great liberating ideas of the Enlightenment or of early Marxism); at the other extreme, however, lies the

incoherence of purely individual and emotional disenchantment with the world, or the self-righteous moralizing
cant which is the preferred mode of expression of some
young radicals. In the last few years some of the common
ideas which have appeared in the social movements have
been more closely examined, and there have been some
attempts to elaborate a social theory which would take account of the new radicalism and its aims.[10] "Participatory
democracy," for example, which in one aspect seems
merely to express the comradeship experienced in the social movements (like that of the Left Book Clubs and the
youth movements in the 1930s), does also propose, as I
suggested earlier, an alternative to the mass society; it has
obvious affinities with the philosophical socialism of the
young Marx, as this has been expounded in recent years;
and it is relevant to such experiments in social participation as workers' self-management, communities of work,
and community development projects. The aims and the
practices of radical social movements could, and should,
provide much more of the empirical material for a theory
of society—as they did in the nineteenth century—and to
the extent that this is happening, that sociologists are pay-
ing more attention to movements of opposition in the
industrial societies and to revolutionary movements in the
developing countries, so the prospects for a more systematic body of critical social thought improve.

Yet these tentative approaches to a new critical theory
are still very different from the confident and sweeping
interpretations of social events in the 1930s. One reason

[10] One line of endeavor, beginning from the work of C. Wright Mills,
may be seen in the contributions to *The New Sociology*, edited by Irving
L. Horowitz (1964). Another is to be found in the proceedings of the
Socialist Scholars Conference, which promises to become an important
annual gathering of the radical intellectuals.

for the difference is an uncertainty about what it is exactly that the present social movements represent; whether, for example, they are or can become the modern equivalents of the working class, with the kind of role in producing social changes that the latter had in Marx's theoretical scheme. The character of these movements poses indeed an interesting sociological problem. The movements differ, in particular, from most earlier radical movements in being predominantly *youth* movements. They express the aspirations and frustrations of a generation, rather than those of a nation, ethnic group or social class; even in the Negro revolt (and also in the Quebec nationalist movement) there is an emphasis upon generational differences as well as a high proportion of youthful leaders. It is true, of course, that social movements, whether radical or conservative, have usually had youth movements associated with them, and that they have sometimes used the symbolism of youth in their campaigns—Mazzini's "young Italy" and Disraeli's "young England" are notable examples. But I doubt if there has been, in any earlier movements, such an unalloyed preoccupation with and insistence upon the differences between generations. The slogan "Don't trust anyone over thirty," which the student movement produced, may have reflected a passing mood, provoked by the defection of middle-aged liberal intellectuals during the McCarthy era; but the dress, the style, the language of the movements all continue to emphasize their youthful character. "Make love, not war" is hardly an exhortation directed to the elderly. The fact that the radical movements are animated and led for the most part by university students is itself enough to establish that they are primarily manifestations of a generational culture.

The influence of new generations in bringing about

changes in society, which is so relevant here, has been examined much less fully than have other aspects of social development. Karl Mannheim, in one of the major studies of this question,[11] observes that the succession of generations in human societies means that there is regularly a "fresh contact" with the accumulated heritage, ". . . a novel approach in assimilating, using and developing the proffered material."[12] He notes also the similarities between social classes and age groups, which have in common that ". . . both endow the individuals sharing in them with a common location in the social and historical process, . . . predisposing them for a certain characteristic mode of thought and experience . . ."[13] In periods of rapid social change a new generation is likely to develop a more distinctive outlook and aims, and to come into more acute conflict with the older generations. On the other side Mannheim points out that the unity of a generation is not primarily of the kind which leads to the formation of an actual social group, that the "fresh contact" which new generations enjoy does not imply that their views will be "radical,"[14] and that generation is only one of the factors

[11] Karl Mannheim, "The Problem of Generations" in *Essays on the Sociology of Knowledge,* pp. 276–322.

[12] op. cit. p. 293.

[13] op. cit. p. 291.

[14] op. cit. p. 297 footnote: "It must be emphasized that this 'ability to start afresh' of which we are speaking has nothing to do with 'conservative' and 'progressive' in the usual sense of these terms. Nothing is more false than the usual assumption uncritically shared by most students of generations, that the younger generation is 'progressive' and the older generation *eo ipso* 'conservative.'" Leon Trotsky made a similar comment, with a more Marxist emphasis, in an essay on "The Intelligentsia and Socialism" (1910); after describing the diverse political attitudes of student movements he wrote: "Here we have militant idealism . . . which is characteristic not of a class or of an idea but of an age group; on the other hand, the political content of this idealism is entirely determined by the historical spirit of those classes from which the students come and to which they return."

which determine historical changes, others being the economic, political, ethnic, etc. The significance of generations in the historical process has thus to be investigated for each particular age and place.

It is a vital part of any critical social theory that it should not only analyze the ills of present society and adumbrate the form of an emerging social order, but should also identify the forces which are capable of bringing that new social order into being. The great strength of Marxism has been that it accomplishes all these things, at least in relation to the social struggles in Europe during the later nineteenth century. C. Wright Mills, having rejected the Marxist view of the social role of the working class as an unrealistic one in the conditions of the mid-twentieth century, was obliged to look for other social groups which would be capable of bringing about the radical social changes which he desired. In the end he settled upon the intellectuals and students, though with many doubts about the likelihood that American intellectuals would ever become a radical force. Implicitly he took the view of Schumpeter that the main assault upon capitalism would be one directed against its cultural manifestations, by the intellectuals. Some recent critics, in the student movement itself, have proposed a more direct substitution of students for the proletariat as the animators of social change; arguing, for example, that students are "trainees" for the new working class—not for the new middle class—and that this position in society, together with their experiences of the "knowledge factory," will produce in them a radical consciousness similar to that which devel-

[15] See the discussion by Gregory Calvert, national secretary of Students for a Democratic Society, in the *National Guardian*, March 25, 1967, pp. 3–4.

oped among industrial workers in the nineteenth century.[15]

Few critics have given much attention to the generational character of the social movements, or to the limitations which this character implies. The changes which new generations effect are mainly in the cultural sphere, in the creation of new styles of art, of dress, of talking and living. They do not influence directly the fundamental structure of society—the economy, the property system, the political regime. One reason for this is the mobile and unstable nature of generational groups, which may be contrasted in this respect with social classes. Sociologists have often made the point that a high degree of mobility between classes— or even the appearance of it—is likely to impede the development of class consciousness and of lasting political organizations. Generational groups are by their nature impermanent and their members mobile: no one remains a teenager for very long. Thus, in the case of student movements the rapid circulation of members makes possible equally rapid changes of mood and activity. For the student movement in the U.S.A. to become an enduring radical force it would be necessary that the present radicalism should be handed on intact to each new generation of students over a fairly long period of time (and this depends upon many other factors in the society at large), and that students, after leaving the university, could be inducted into other radical movements—a labor movement, or a progressive intelligentsia—which, however, do not yet exist.

The social movements have achieved a great deal. They have forced attention upon some major evils of American society; they have provoked a spate of social criticism. But no one would claim that they have yet accomplished, or are on the verge of accomplishing, any profound changes in American society. Representing as they do an ethnic group which is a permanent small minority in the population, and the diverse groups which have arisen from a generation more or less confusedly in revolt, they illustrate again, even though they may be slowly overcoming, one of the weaknesses of American radicalism—its lack of a reliable and enduring social basis. It is this fact, beside the intellectual complexities which now beset the social critic, which goes far to explain the hesitancy and unsureness in the voice of dissent.

CHAPTER 7

SOCIALISM
AND
NATIONALISM
IN CANADA

The two most important radical movements in present day Canada are the socialist movement, represented mainly by the New Democratic Party, and the movement in Quebec which has linked socialism with nationalism. I mentioned briefly in an earlier chapter the emergence, in the 1930s, of two opposition movements—the Social Credit Party and the Co-operative Commonwealth Federation—

both of which were responses to the economic depression. The Social Credit movement was inspired originally by the ideas of Major C. H. Douglas, which were grafted on to the existing political movement of the United Farmers of Alberta. Douglas's social doctrines, which he began to expound in England in 1917, belong generally with the theories of technocracy. They have some affinity with the views presented later by Howard Scott, and more elaborately by James Burnham in *The Managerial Revolution*, but they are much more naive, and they include a number of distinctive economic ideas, particularly on the use of the credit system to create in practice the mass prosperity made possible by modern technology.

Douglas's theories were meant to apply to the conditions in an industrial, urban society. Their adoption by a section of the United Farmers of Alberta—an agrarian populist movement—was somewhat incongruous, but in the event this did not matter, since the theories had practically no influence upon policy when the Social Credit party came to power. At the present time the influence of the original ideas is negligible in the Social Credit movement, whether in Alberta, in British Columbia, or in Quebec. The Social Credit parties appear increasingly non-ideological, in the American style, and almost destitute of any ideas, although there remain in them some vestiges of the early technocratic and populist beliefs. Their most obvious characteristic, resulting from the fact that they are parties based upon a few provinces, without any considerable support in the country as a whole, is that they are more inclined than the national parties to emphasize provincial rights; and in Quebec this tendency is reinforced by the prevailing nationalist sentiment.

Lacking any well-formulated theory, or any significant

exposition of a doctrine, the postwar Social Credit movement has contributed little directly to social criticism. What it has done is to pose, by its mere existence, a number of questions about the social influences upon Canadian politics, which have led social scientists to undertake some important critical studies. Among these the outstanding work is C. B. Macpherson's *Democracy in Alberta: Social Credit and the Party System* (1953, 2nd. edn. 1962). Professor Macpherson investigates very thoroughly the origins of the Alberta Social Credit movement in agrarian radicalism, the plebiscitarian character of its rule, and the implications of this for a democratic system. He also considers possible explanations of the oscillation between radicalism and conservatism in Alberta politics, and indicates a likely cause in the fluctuating economic situation of farmers—or rather, of the different categories of farmers—who are in varying degrees independent entrepreneurs and yet dependent upon eastern financiers. When the farmers feel most secure in their entrepreneurial role their outlook is conservative; when their independence is threatened, as during the depression, they become radical. The Social Credit movement in British Columbia received its initial impetus from Alberta, but it developed in very different circumstances, during the prosperity of the 1950s and as an effective adversary of socialism in the province. Unlike the Alberta movement it does not have its source in agrarian radicalism; it began rather as a party of the small businessmen and the conservative farmers, achieving its success as a result of the failure of the old right-wing parties, and by riding and managing the economic boom.[1]

C. B. Macpherson's study brings to light, in a particular

---

[1] See Martin Robin, "The Social Basis of Party Politics in British Columbia," in Hugh G. Thorburn (editor), *Party Politics in Canada* (Scarborough, 1967), pp. 201–211.

context, the connections between economic circumstances, class position and political action, which have become increasingly prominent in recent social criticism. The development of the socialist movement in Canada has an important place here; for as a political movement it raises in practice the problem of class differences, while as the source and the vehicle of expression of an ideology it promotes a systematic criticism of the state of society. Canadian socialism, as an influential national movement, dates from the 1930s when the Co-operative Commonwealth Federation was formed. From the outset it was influenced strongly by the ideas of British socialism, as earlier labor movements in Canada had been. Its program, as set out in the Regina Manifesto (1933), resembles that of the Labor Party; its social doctrine is expounded more elaborately in a volume entitled *Social Planning for Canada* (1935) produced by the League for Social Reconstruction, which played a similar role to that of the Fabian Society in Britain although it did not have anything like the same eminence. The socialist aims of the C.C.F., and the need for social planning, were reaffirmed in the Winnipeg Declaration of Principles (1956), but in a language which reflected those postwar changes in the western societies—Canada among them—that we associate with sustained economic growth, full employment, and the development of a "Welfare State."

In 1958 the C.C.F. responded to a resolution of the Canadian Labor Congress which urged the creation of a new political movement; a Joint National Committee of the C.C.F. and C.L.C. was formed to discuss the proposal; and in 1961 the New Democratic Party was founded with the support of socialist groups and trade unions.[2] In the same year a new exposition of socialist ideas was published

[2] See Stanley Knowles, *The New Party* (Toronto, 1961).

under the title *Social Purpose for Canada*.[3] This work does not differ fundamentally, in its criticism of Canadian society, from the book published by the League for Social Reconstruction in 1935; but its approach and its terminology are adapted to the new conditions of the 1960s. *Social Planning for Canada* had to deal with the apparent economic collapse of capitalism in the depression and with the dramatic confrontation between two worlds which the rise of national socialism in Germany projected upon the international scene; it put forward as a solution for the crisis the socialist planning of the economy. It belonged to the period, and to some extent shared the mood, of the Left Book Club in Britain, and of those critics in the United States who produced *Culture and the Crisis*, or who attempted to create a third party.

Social Purpose for Canada deals with the prosperous, partially planned, "welfare" capitalist society of the 1950s. Its themes are the need to spread more widely the newly gained affluence and especially to direct more resources to the improvement of public amenities; to control the massive and concentrated power which results from the rise of large business corporations; and to define more clearly the character, the prospects, and the aims of Canadian society. The last is an almost wholly new concern of social criticism, expressed in the continuing, sometimes tedious, discussions of "Canadian identity." But of course this is not only a Canadian problem. In all the industrial societies, as I have suggested, there is a widespread uneasiness about the kind of society that is being created by mass production and automation, by affluence and increasing leisure; and at the same time there is profound uncertainty about the principles which should, or could, guide men in shaping their future society. The younger generation, in many

---

[3] Michael Oliver (editor), *Social Purpose for Canada* (Toronto, 1961).

countries, is in revolt against the old order, but does not offer any clear vision of a new order. The situation is similar, with perhaps a greater gulf between the generations, in the developing countries; and in some respects Canada might be regarded as a "new nation"—the debate about "Canadian identity" resembling that about the "African personality"—which has only now become aware of its unique social structure and problems, and of its possible role in the world. Many of these problems, however, loom larger in Canada because of the diversity of the influences which have been at work here, coming from Britain, from France, and from the United States; and the consequent difficulty of bringing disparate social conceptions together in a single coherent view of the future.

If social criticism in Canada is compared with that in the United States at the present time, it is evident that the former enjoys in one respect an advantage by being closely associated with a political movement which endows it with some consistency, continuity and mass appeal. The New Democratic Party is an urban working-class party, like the European Socialist parties, and it has become well established as the third party in Canadian national politics.[4] Its achievement is due in part to the fact that it continues the successful prewar socialist movement, which reached its high point in 1943-44 when the C.C.F. took the lead in popular support for a short time,[5] gained more than a third of the seats in the Ontario legislature, and formed the government in Saskatchewan after winning 47 of the 52 seats in the legislature. By contrast, most of the move-

[4] Its share of the vote in federal elections has steadily increased, reaching 18 per cent in 1965, although it still has only 21 members out of the 265 in the House of Commons.

[5] The National Gallup poll of September 1943 showed the C.C.F. receiving the support of 29 per cent of the population while the liberal and conservative parties each received 28 per cent.

ments of the 1930s in the U.S.A. failed to survive the New Deal and the war; and the present generation of radicals disavows explicitly any attachment to them. Some writers have questioned the radicalism of Canadian socialism,[6] but in doing so they have taken too little account of the extent to which revisionism has been forced upon most left-wing parties since the war, and also of the peculiar difficulties which face a labor movement in North America. The N.D.P. does provide, at least, a meeting place for radical intellectuals, politicians and trade union leaders, and it forms, like the British Labour Party, a center from which a variety of criticisms of society can emanate. As the only effective socialist movement to emerge in North America it will have an opportunity in the next decade to exert a major influence upon the course of social criticism on this continent.

Other factors, however, detract somewhat from this advantage. A vital tradition of social criticism does not exist in Canada, and there has always been a strong temptation simply to adopt the style and the issues of foreign critics. This is quite obvious in the present social movements, which are inclined to imitate, sometimes inappropriately, those of the United States, and to be concerned much more with the problems of American society than with their own.[7] It is difficult, no doubt, to escape this condition in view of the tremendous economic and cultural influence of the United States, and when even the opposition to that influence may lead to the same preoccupation with American affairs. The way out of this difficulty, I think, will be

[6] See, for example, Leo Zakuta, *A Protest Movement Becalmed: A Study of Change in the CCF* (Toronto, 1964).

[7] In the past year or two, however, the Student Union for Peace Action (S.U.P.A.) has been active in many local projects concerned with poverty and economic backwardness.

for Canadian socialism, and social criticism generally, to affirm more strongly its European connections, and to present in a more compelling fashion the idea of Canada as a European nation in North America.[8]

The second of the movements which animate social criticism in Canada, the Quebec nationalist movement, adds another line of division, between ethnic groups, to that between Left and Right. When Everett Hughes concluded his study of *French Canada in Transition* in the early 1940s he referred to "the development of the modern industrial economy, including the American type of urban life and institutions," "their threat to the old French economy," and "the unsatisfactory place of French-Canadians in the newer economic system," as being responsible for the dissatisfaction, the revolts, and the rising nationalism in French Canada. In the past twenty years the economic changes have proceeded apace, and their effects have been studied extensively by French-Canadian social scientists. Two recent publications provide a useful conspectus of the social transformations in French Canada, and of the new doctrines and criticisms which have appeared since the war. One is the volume of essays edited by Marcel Rioux and Yves Martin under the title *French-Canadian Society* (1964); the other a collection of four articles published in a French sociological journal, the *Cahiers internationaux de sociologie,* in 1965.[9] The authors of these various

[8] A similar argument is presented from the European side in Claude Julien, *Le Canada, dernière chance de l'Europe* (Paris, 1965).

[9] *Cahiers internationaux de sociologie,* Vol. XXXVIII, 1965. Fernand Dumont, *"La représentation idéologique des classes au Canada français,"* pp. 85–98; Marcel Rioux, *"Conscience nationale et conscience de classe au Québec,"* pp. 99–108; Jean-Charles Falardeau, *"L'Origine et l'ascension des hommes d'affaires dans la société Canadienne-Française,"* pp. 109–120; Gérald Fortin, *"Milieu rural et milieu ouvrier: deux classes virtuelles,"* pp. 121–130.

papers would agree that the major fact in the recent history of Quebec is the extremely rapid industrialization and urbanization. In less than forty years the urban population has grown from 40 per cent to 70 per cent of the total population. Agricultural workers, who made up a quarter of the employed population twenty years ago now account for only 6 per cent. The tertiary sector of the economy, comprising commercial and service occupations, has grown remarkably, and now accounts for more than half the employed population.

Largely as a result of these changes the outlook of French Canadians—their conception of themselves and of their society—has been profoundly altered. Marcel Rioux, in the paper which he contributes to the *Cahiers internationaux de sociologie,* emphasizes this evolution in the self-image of the people of Quebec. From considering themselves as a cultural group, the bearers of a traditional way of life, they have come to see themselves as an industrial society, and the government of Quebec as the government of their nation state. Rioux draws attention in several ways to the extension and the growing intensity of national sentiment. For example, a study which he made of the views of young people showed that while socialist ideas were quite widely diffused, no one was a socialist without being a nationalist, and in the group as a whole national consciousness predominated very clearly over class consciousness. Fernand Dumont emphasizes more strongly the socialist element in his essay on the ideological representation of classes. The dominant ideology in French Canada from 1850 to 1950 was always nationalism; but the idea of a nation, in this period, was based upon images derived from an earlier rural society. Recent nationalism has a different character;

it tends to identify the nation with the working class. This account formulates an association between nationalist and socialist ideas which is evident in much French-Canadian social criticism. But the association is far from complete. Even in the separatist movement, organized since 1960 mainly in the *Rassemblement pour l'indépendance nationale* (R.I.N.), there have been divisions between the socialists and the more conservative nationalists, although one of its leaders asserts that the movement as a whole has now ". . . recognized the necessity of associating national liberation with the transformation of society."[10]

It is primarily the group associated with the journal *Parti pris* who see a necessary connection between nationalism and socialism, resulting from two conditions: first, the growth of a vigorous working-class movement in the course of industrialization; and secondly, the colonial situation of the working class in relation to the economic dominance of English-Canadian and American business. Essentially, they argue that the nationalist movement in Quebec has the same social bases and character as the independence movements in former colonial countries in Asia and Africa, or in Cuba, in which there was also a merging of socialist and nationalist ideas. But the analogy has been presented only in vague terms,[11] without a rigorous examination of the resemblances and differences between the social movements in Quebec and colonial independence movements. In my view the differences—economic, political and cultural—are by far the more striking. A better analogy for the French-Canadian situation would be, perhaps, the position of one of the national minorities in the old

[10] André d'Allemagne, *Le colonialisme au Québec* (Montreal, 1966) p. 170.

[11] For example, in André d'Allemagne, op. cit.

Austro-Hungarian Empire; and a socialist critic might turn with advantage to some of the writings on the question of nationalities by the Austro-Marxists,[12] who noted the possible conflict between the doctrines of nationalism and socialism.

The separatists form only a small minority within the nationalist movement at the present time, but their ideas have had an important influence in stimulating the demand for greater independence. This independence is conceived in a variety of ways, ranging from an extension of provincial autonomy to the formation of a separate French-Canadian state. In November 1966 preliminary sittings of an "Estates-General of French Canada" were held in Montreal, with the intention of bringing together different sections of the nationalist movement to study the present condition of the French-Canadian nation, to define its objectives, and to undertake action which would achieve its aspirations. The report of the conference makes clear that constitutional reforms are envisaged which would result in a more autonomous Quebec government. Similarly, the claims of the recently elected *Union Nationale* government in Quebec for greater independence in foreign relations seem to imply constitutional changes of some importance.

Within the nationalist movement socialism, like separatism, is still a subordinate current of opinion. It is true that the new nationalism is in part a creation of working-class organizations, and also that socialist ideas have spread widely among the younger generation (as in the case of the American social movements). But Quebec nationalism is also, and perhaps mainly, the ideology of the new urban

---

[12] The classical work is Otto Bauer, *Die Nationalitätenfrage und die Sozialdemokratie* (Vienna, 1907).

middle class, of professional men, managers, technicians, who are not predominantly socialist in their outlook. The present association between socialism and nationalism in some sections of the social movement in Quebec is, in my view, unstable and unlikely to last. In that case, two possible outcomes may be envisaged. One is that socialism will gain the ascendancy, that an alliance will be formed between the socialist movements of English and French Canada, and that social criticism will be mainly concerned with the "social question"—with class, equality, poverty, public ownership. The other is that nationalism will triumph and that the overriding social issue of the 1970s will be whether Canada is to be one nation or two.

The second alternative appears perhaps more likely at the present time, if we consider the vigor of the nationalist movement in Quebec and the extent to which the cultural differences between English and French Canada seem to have been accentuated rather than diminished in recent years, in spite of the tentative steps towards bilingualism. The social sciences themselves provide an odd confirmation of this tendency. French-Canadian sociologists have produced, during the past decade, an impressive number of studies of their society, which both reflect and contribute to a greater awareness of its changes and problems. Their studies, particularly when they deal with social stratification, display very plainly the influence of French ideas and terminology; those, for example, of the late Professor Gurvitch, and of Sartre's methodological treatise, *Critique de la raison dialectique*. In English-speaking Canada, however, the main influence has come from American sociology, and social thought is indebted for much of its language and concepts to the writings of Parsons and Merton on one side, Mills and Riesman on the other. I will not venture to judge exactly how much traffic there is across this linguistic and cultural line; but many indications, including the published literature, suggest that it is inconsiderable and that there exist two largely separate worlds of thought and criticism at the present time. Even the left-wing journals of opinion seem to be confined within their ethnic region; *Canadian Dimension,* the voice of the New Left in English Canada, rarely discusses the social movements and ideas in Quebec, while *Parti pris* largely ignores English-Canadian socialism.

In spite of this, however, the issues which are raised by the socialist movement and by the French-Canadian nationalist movement are not altogether dissimilar. One preeminent problem is that concerning the nature and degree of social stratification, of domination and subjection, in Canada; and it is not surprising, therefore, that a major work of recent Canadian sociology, which is also an important contribution to social criticism—John Porter's *The Vertical Mosaic* (1965)—should be devoted to this subject. Porter's book, which follows in a different style the line of investigation and criticism opened up by C. Wright Mills in *The Power Elite,* has as one of its main themes the contrast between the actual distribution of wealth and power in Canada, and what the author terms the "persistent image" that Canadians have of their society as being "classless" and egalitarian. This image, which is similar to the one which Americans have, or have had, of *their* society, is explicable by some very similar historical antecedents; for example, the settlement of a frontier, which established a rough kind of equality among pioneer farmers. There are other important similarities, and notably the way in which ethnic diversity has tended to overshadow class differences and to obstruct the development of social movements based upon class interest; as it does most strikingly at present through the distinction between French and English in Canada, Negro and white in the United States.

The major part of Porter's book is devoted to showing exactly how inegalitarian Canadian society is, in the distribution of wealth, and in the opportunities for education, for social mobility, or for access to political power. It shows at the same time the important part which ethnic origins and religious affiliations have played in determining an individual's place in the social hierarchy. Porter concludes that Canada, as a new country, should have had great opportunities for social innovation, but that it has not so far taken advantage of them. In his words, "a fragmented political structure, a lack of upward mobility into its elite and higher occupational levels, and the absence of a clearly articulated system of values," are among the reasons for Canada's retardation. Canadian society still appears as an adaptation of its British and French founding groups, rather than as a new breed in a new nation.

But these may not be quite the proper conclusions to draw about the Canadian class structure. Canada did not become, so rapidly as did the United States, a wealthy country in which great fortunes were made. There is no occasion for Porter in his book to investigate the history of the great *Canadian* fortunes (since they have no history), or to examine the formation of an upper class by the families of the very rich, as did Mills in his study of the U.S.A. Prosperity and wealth on the American scale have come since the war, and the problems they raise are those of the economic power of large corporations (often American corporations) rather than, at this stage, the power of inherited family wealth. Canada, one might say, is just about ready for its progressive movement and its muckraking era. But this would ignore the other circumstances which make the 1960s so different from the 1900s, and Canada itself so different from the United States.[18] The great accumulation of wealth is taking place in a post-New Deal, post-Welfare State age, when wealth no longer stands in such a dramatic contrast with extreme poverty. Again, Canadian municipal government and administration, because it was so much influenced by that in Britain and France, has never presented the kind of problem which Lincoln Steffens dealt with in his articles on "the shame of the cities." What is left for the Canadian muckraker is principally the investigation of the great corporations, which Porter has usefully begun in his book.

The problems of inherited wealth and a more clearly articulated class system may come to surpass in importance the problems of ethnic division in the next few decades. In my opinion, they are of more fundamental importance. Even the present impassioned concern with the cultural differences and social inequalities between English and French, does perhaps show a dawning awareness that these are problems within a Canadian society which faces many other difficulties and opportunities. It is arguable that notwithstanding the present vigor of Quebec nationalism the "two nations" of the English and the French were most separate and distinct in the period before the agitations of the last two decades; the one, rural, traditional, withdrawn and acquiescent, the other commercial, modern and politically dominant, living side by side for much of the time in mutual ignorance and disregard. Now they are both industrial and urban societies, by no means so separate in eco-

---

[18] In Western Canada there are still some manifestations of the robber baron mentality, but the social context is quite different.

nomic and political affairs, and culturally diverse only within a *modern* culture, which is nourished in one case mainly by Britain and the United States, in the other mainly by France; a culture which has probably fewer significant elements of division in it than were produced earlier by the pre-eminent differences in religion and in economic activity. English and French Canadians do inhabit different cultural worlds—even, as I have indicated, within the social sciences—but it does not follow that they must of necessity be engaged in ideological conflict; or on the other side that they are likely to be unaware of, or indifferent to, each other. There are many other affiliations, of economic interest, of class and politics, which traverse the cultural frontier. The prominence which Porter gives to ethnic diversity, and particularly to the division between English and French Canada—for instance, in his references to the "dual loyalties which prevent the emergence of any clear Canadian identity"—although it has a historical justification does seem to neglect unduly the modern development of a more clearly perceived class structure and of social movements which reflect this change. In one respect his book itself exemplifies the traditional English-Canadian view of the mosaic character of Canadian society; for in this work of more than six hundred pages on social class and power in Canada the forty pages or so which deal with French Canada hardly mention its class structure and draw upon few of the important recent studies by French-Canadian social scientists.

These two social movements—socialism and Quebec nationalism—are today the principal sources and animators of radical social thought in Canada. What prospects do they hold out for the future development of social criticism? I noted earlier that the critic in Canada has some advantage over his American counterpart in the possibility of associating himself with an established and ongoing political movement, but that there are also disadvantages in the lack of a critical tradition, the absence of any outstanding earlier schools of social thought with which he can identify himself in his own country. His sources lie, for the most part, outside Canada. There is still no intellectual center, certainly no intellectual establishment such as exists in the United States; the journals of opinion are few, and they are, with some exceptions, insipid and dull. On the other hand there is in Canada still relatively little of that anti-intellectualism—the direct hostility to intellect—what drives the American critic into isolation, cuts him off from the main currents of American life, and occasionally sends him into exile in Europe, as it is beginning to do once again in the 1960s. The social movements provide the intellectual critic in Canada with a recognized arena for controversy and with a place where he can participate genuinely in the life of his society.

For the present, the development of social ideas proceeds in two separate streams, English and French. Of these, it seems to me, the French is more lively in its social criticism and has come nearer to creating an original school of social thought. This is explicable by the more rapid and exciting changes which have been taking place in French-Canadian society; and to a lesser extent, perhaps, by the influence of French intellectuals, themselves more deeply committed to distinctive ideologies than are intellectuals in Britain or the United States. If in the coming years these two streams were to converge or merge there might develop a more vigorous Canadian style of social criticism. It would not lack issues to attack: the problems arising from the consolidation of a new structure of class and power; the question of nationalities; the character of Canadian politics (following the lines of C. B. Macpherson's pioneer study); the influence of the United States, viewed in relation to Canada's links with Europe; poverty, especially among the Indians, and among some immigrant groups; the need to provide more extensively for education and recreation; the reform of university government; the challenge of urban and regional planning. In the older parties the exhaustion of political ideas is evident.[14] The socialist movement may possibly become an outlet for the energies and ideas of a much more critical younger generation, and so prepare the ground for a new growth of social thought. The signs are not yet clear. Above all, Canada still lives too much in the shadow of the United States.

[14] An exception should be made for Walter Gordon whose book *A Choice For Canada* deals in a lively and trenchant manner with some important current issues.

C H A P T E R 8

CRITICISM

AND

IDEOLOGY

Social criticism is not science, but in modern times it has been very much dependent upon the social sciences. In earlier ages it was often religious movements—the "religions of the oppressed" as they have been called—which led the way in social criticism. Somewhat later it was the schools of philosophy which largely assumed this role in Europe. But from the end of the eighteenth century most of the movements of criticism were based upon some theory of society. The Utilitarians, the Saint-Simonians,

Comte and the positivists, the various schools of socialism, and especially Marxism, all combined in their teaching a theory about the nature of human society, a criticism of contemporary society, and a plan for its reorganization.

During the nineteenth century social criticism became broader and deeper than it had ever been before, and there was hardly a field of intellectual endeavor which was not affected by it. The culture of the European societies was transformed and became divided between conflicting ideologies, as Raymond Williams has shown most clearly, taking the example of Britain, in his book *Culture and Society*. Novelists, dramatists, and literary critics were diverted to new themes and they became as much concerned as were the social thinkers with the rise of industry, the growth of towns, the development of working-class movements, the progress of democracy, and the turmoil of discordant world views. This intellectual ferment of the latter part of the nineteenth century reached a climax in the 1930s with the depression and the outbreak of the Second World War. Since then we have entered, it might be said, a new age in which the tremendous advances of natural science confront us with nuclear war, automation, and the exploration of space, with the vision of immensely wealthy societies and the immediate difficulties of a population explosion; and in which the problem of social classes begins to assume a new form, as a matter of sharing power and responsibility, and of asserting the claims of the public good, or civilized life, against reckless private indulgence, in place of the earlier stark confrontation between wealth and poverty.

In the United States social criticism has rarely been either so comprehensive or so profound as in Europe. The founding fathers in the eighteenth century, the transcendental thinkers of the 1840s, propounded doctrines in which there is a recognizable unity of view. Even more, the progressive era at the beginning of this century had a distinctive intellectual character, but its most eminent thinkers—Dewey, Veblen, Holmes and Beard—were less closely associated, and had almost certainly a less marked influence upon the general culture, than was the case with similar groups of intellectuals in France, Britain, or Germany in the same period. Only in the 1930s did there emerge, for a time, a broader critical movement which appeared capable of bringing together diverse groups in the intellectual community. Even then, as I suggested earlier, it was the literary intellectuals—writers and critics such as Upton Sinclair, Dos Passos, Edmund Wilson, Granville Hicks—who led the way, without much support from social theorists. They were living, in fact, on borrowed Marxism.

Throughout this study, while examining the ideas of American critics in different periods, I have also been concerned with the general question as to why they have not had a greater social and political influence. In part, I have suggested, it is because they have not had a wide enough audience, in the absence of any organized and enduring movement of political protest and opposition which would be receptive to their ideas. However, a number of recent writers have laid greater weight upon what they see as a strain of anti-intellectualism in American society. This is a major theme of Jacques Barzun's *The House of Intellect,* and it is the subject of a thorough historical examination in Richard Hofstadter's recent book *Anti-Intellectualism in American Life.* Hofstadter surveys a great number of examples of hostility and opposition to the intellectual life, culminating in the fever of McCarthyism in the 1950s, with its introduction and extensive use of the pejorative term "egghead." (This, by the way, reproduces exactly Napoleon Bonaparte's use of the term "ideologist" to describe the intellectual critics of his imperial rule.) Hofstadter quotes, among recent examples of this anti-intellectual outlook, Louis Bromfield's definition of an egghead, which begins: "A person of spurious intellectual pretensions . . . fundamentally superficial . . . over-emotional and feminine in reactions to any problems," and concludes with a judgment on ". . . the extreme remoteness of the 'egghead' from the thought and feeling of the whole of the people." The number and variety of Hofstadter's examples, which it would be difficult to equal from any European country (or from Canada), suggests that anti-intellectualism as a persistent and widespread phenomenon is uniquely American. Of course, it has appeared in a sporadic and partial fashion in other societies; in France under Napoleon, and again at the time of the Dreyfus affair, and in Britain among the squirearchy of the nineteenth century; but it does not seem to have attained anywhere else the intensity and durability which it has had in the United States. Often enough, in the European countries, the criticism of intellectuals has come from other intellectuals. France provides two excellent examples, in Julien Benda's *The Betrayal of the Intellectuals*, which criticizes them for succumbing to the passions of the market place; and in Raymond Aron's *The Opium of the Intellectuals*, which renews the criticism in the circumstances of the 1950s when some French intellectuals, in his view, had forsaken the standards of dispassionate criticism in their assessment of Soviet Marxism.

Anti-intellectualism in the United States shows itself in another aspect in the relatively small place which intellectuals have occupied in the major political parties. They have taken part in radical movements, and they have sometimes been drawn into the work of government as members of a "brain trust," as in the administrations of Roosevelt and Kennedy, but they have not usually had much prominence in the councils of the parties themselves; certainly not as much as in European political parties, and especially those of the Left, in which intellectuals were very often the most prominent leaders. Intellectual critics in the United States have only intermittently found a political movement with which they could identify themselves; the established parties have only occasionally thought it important to gain the allegiance of intellectual groups.

Besides this anti-intellectualism which inhibits criticism by diminishing the confidence and self-regard of the intellectuals, and by excluding them from practical life, two more general influences have affected the nature of recent social criticism in the United States, as in most other western countries. The first may be described briefly as a revolt against rationalism. About the end of the nineteenth century there appeared in the European countries several new doctrines which challenged the supremacy of reason, as against feeling, in human life; criticized those theories which explained social events in terms of rational motives; and declared their opposition to the trend of the modern societies toward a more rational, technological and industrial way of life. These various elements occurred in different proportions in particular doctrines. A sociologist such as Max Weber saw rationality as the principal and growing influence in modern social life, but he deplored its consequences in the inexorable spread of bureaucracy and in the "disenchantment of the world." His contemporary, Pareto, was just as convinced that reason played a minor part in the affairs of society, which were directed in the main by powerful innate sentiments or emotional predispositions, and were merely overlaid by the rationalistic doctrines which sought to account for them. In this same period, Bergson, in France, propounded a philosophy in which a mysterious "vital impulse" replaced intellect as the motive power in human affairs, and Sorel translated this into a social theory which stressed the influence of irrational myths and of violence in accomplishing social changes. Freud, in some respects the most influential of all these thinkers, although himself a rationalist, gave currency to ideas which could be interpreted as meaning that human life, both individual and social, was unalterably beneath the sway of non-rational, and possibly irrational, impulses.

This reorientation of European social thought, which H. Stuart Hughes has described admirably in his *Consciousness and Society*, produced three major consequences. First, it bred scepticism about the validity of any general theory of society. Secondly, it engendered a revulsion against the whole industrial way of life. Thirdly, it reintroduced the idea of a contrast and potential opposition between intellect and feeling in human life, and took sides with the latter. As Hughes observes, these thinkers— Pareto, Weber, Bergson, Sorel, Freud and many others whose influence was less dramatic—"were all in their different ways striving to comprehend the newly recognized disparity between external reality and the internal appreciation of that reality." They were all intensely aware of the subjective nature of social thought, and while some of them searched for a new objective basis for social theory, others accepted, cheerfully or despairingly as the case might be, that any interpretation of man's history and social life had to be based upon an "intuition." The recent progeny of this view are numerous, ranging from new Hegelian versions of Marxism to the varieties of existentialist social philosophy, and they help to shape the undogmatic, highly personal and idiosyncratic social criticism of the present time.

The revulsion against industrialism and technology has taken many forms, in Spengler's philosophy of history, in D. H. Lawrence's denunciation of the ugly soulless life of industrial England, in Huxley's ironical look at the *Brave New World,* in the sustained criticism of modern urban life by Lewis Mumford. Often it has been associated with the distinction between intellect and feeling as elements in social life, and with praise of a more spontaneous, emotional and active mode of life. This is not anti-intellectualism in the sense which I described earlier; that is, it is not an opposition to the life of the mind as such, although it may sometimes verge upon it. It proclaims rather, a romantic ideal of a life of action in which intellect and feeling would come into a harmonious relationship; its symbols are the philosophical gamekeeper, or the bullfighter, not the successful and conforming "organization man" with his suburban home and his piece of Californian real estate. In our own time, the beatniks express most forcefully, though with less art, the hostility to industrialism and to that form of rationality in the modern world which finds its ultimate end in purely economic success.[1]

---

[1] Their protest is also a *postwar* phenomenon, and it re-enacts earlier demonstrations; for instance, that of the 1920s of which Stephen Spender wrote: "The tiredness of our generation consists in exploring unimportant and superficial aspects of the idea of freedom . . . Freedom, the young people in Hamburg said, is sexual freedom primarily, then freedom to enjoy yourself, to wander, not to make money, not to have the responsibility of a family, or the duties of a citizen, generally. Freedom is one long holiday. They were tired. What they wanted, in fact, was a holiday." *Partisan Review* VII (2) 1940, p. 102.

The second general influence upon modern criticism is social rather than intellectual. It consists in the growth in numbers, diversity and specialization of the intellectual class itself. From the time of the Enlightenment until well into the nineteenth century the intellectuals—in the narrow sense of those who create and diffuse ideas and cultural symbols—were a small part of the population in all modern societies, and the body of knowledge with which they dealt could still, in some manner, be encompassed as a whole. Comte and Spencer, and many lesser thinkers, considered themselves justified in surveying the whole range of the sciences and in formulating comprehensive theories of the development of knowledge and of social life. With the rapid growth of knowledge and its increasing specialization during the past hundred years, this kind of universal competence has become impossible. It is not merely that there has grown up the division between the "two cultures" which C. P. Snow has described, but that within each discipline in the sciences and humanities an intensive specialization has taken place. We live, undeniably, in the age of the expert. In the natural sciences this specialization has been, on the whole, fruitful from the point of view of discovery and application. In the social sciences and humanities specialization and expertise are more questionable. Certainly they allow us to get a clearer view of particular aspects of human life, and perhaps to deal more effectively with specific social problems (although the problems seem to multiply at least as fast as the remedies). What they do at the same time, however, is to impede the expression of any comprehensive view of human society, of any general social criticism, or of any broad alternative conception of a new society or civilization.

Opinions may differ on whether any such general views of the human condition are necessary, or whether they need find a place within the social sciences. Karl Popper, for instance, suggests as the practical task of the social sciences, in their critical role, what he calls "social engineering"; that is, the diagnosis and correction of particular social ills within a form of society—western democratic society as it now exists—the main structure of which is to be taken as being no longer in question. On the other side, there are radical critics who see a need for some more comprehensive social doctrine which would shape particular criticisms and reforms to a clearly perceived end, which would lift us out of the present *malaise,* and set us again on the path upon which the thinkers of the Enlightenment and the early socialists embarked so hopefully.

The last great social theory which was able to animate in this fashion a movement of social criticism and reconstruction was Marxism. Stuart Hughes is right, I think, when he says of the thinkers who followed Marx and who brought about the change in European social thought, that they "were haunted by a sense of living in an age of merely derivative philosophy and scholarship"; that although some of them were builders of great inclusive systems, "they narrowed the range through which such general theorizing might operate and cast doubt on the future usefulness of intellectual operations of this type." The philosophy and scholarship of the present generation are still more obviously derivative, the doubts more severe and oppressive. It is still possible to regard Marxism as the social theory which makes the greatest sense out of the confused period in which we live, but it has become more and more difficult to do so as the twentieth century goes on; and the decade of the 1930s marks, in my view, the climax of the achievement of classical Marxism as an explanatory scheme and a guide to action. Among recent thinkers Sartre, especially in his *Critique de la raison dialectique,* has made the largest claims for Marxism: "Far from being worn out," he asserts, "Marxism is still very young, almost in its infancy. It has barely started to develop. It is therefore still the philosophy of our time. It is unsurpassable, because we have not yet passed beyond the circumstances that created it. Our thoughts, whatever they are, can take shape only upon this humus. They must be contained within the framework it provides, or be lost in a vacuum, or retrogress." To criticize in detail Sartre's view, or to examine his own revision of Marxism, which seeks to unite some elements of Marx's thought with some elements of existentialism, would lead far beyond the present subject. Let me observe only that Sartre makes two particularly questionable assertions. The first, that there is a single philosophy of our time, is contradicted by the growing fragmentation of world-views, by widespread scepticism, and by the fierce rejection of ideology in many modern social movements. The second assertion, that we have not yet passed beyond the circumstances which created Marxist thought, appears strange to many sociologists, for whom it is just the extent to which modern societies *have* passed beyond the circumstances of early capitalism, in a century of incredibly rapid change, which accounts for the crisis of Marxist thought in the last three decades.

The majority of social scientists in most countries—in the Soviet societies as well as in the western democracies—have been content until very lately to accept their new role as experts and social engineers. Giving their assent with varying degrees of enthusiasm to an established orthodox view, or tolerated range of views, about the nature of their own society, whatever it may be, they have devoted themselves to expounding the orthodoxy, or to criticizing and proposing reforms in limited areas of social life. They have publicized social ills, and they have served on committees and commissions appointed to set them right. In all this they undoubtedly perform a useful function as critics of modern society. Yet this may not be enough. There may still be a need for criticism of a more general kind, which would examine and question precisely the ruling orthodoxies, the fundamental ideas and institutions of a society, in the manner of the liberal and socialist thinkers in the nineteenth century. To some extent this need was obscured by the clash between the ideologies of nations in the Second World War, and again after the war in the confrontation between the Soviet and western blocs. It has become apparent once more, as some international tensions decline and as others produce divisions within the contending nations. In the Soviet countries Marxism now receives the grudging acquiescence of the intellectuals; it is not enthusiastically embraced as a new vision of the world, or as a new and devastating weapon of criticism. The old-style Marxism is simply boring, and the most vigorous thinkers are engaged in a thoroughgoing revision of Marx's philosophical and sociological ideas. In the western societies the concern with "identity" and "purpose," with theories of industrialization and modernization which serve us in place of the old belief in progress, reveals a desire for some scheme of thought, not to be found ready to hand, which would enable us to interpret more adequately the events of the twentieth century and would provide a surer guide than we now have to private and public action. Of course, the desire may be vain. The new renaissance may not come. We may be obliged to live with our present uncertainties, confronting diverse ways of life and a confusion of social ideals. Perhaps we should be satisfied if our descendants a hundred years hence can say simply: "Mankind has survived." But this is not my own view. The fragmentation of social thought at the present time is explicable in part, I think, by the fact that we have not yet assimilated thoroughly the disturbing ideas and doctrines of Marx and Freud, of Kierkegaard and Nietzsche, and of the lesser thinkers who interpreted their theories. The radical ideas which they originated were diffused very slowly, assumed a variety of forms, and were often appropriated by sects and movements; it is quite recently that the scholarly commentaries upon them have begun to appear. The very growth of the social sciences, which has meant vast additions to the body of knowledge about social life, has increased the difficulty of dealing with such large conceptions as these thinkers produced. It is hard to conceive that a work on the scale of Marx's *Capital* could be undertaken today, however obvious may be the need for an interpretation of the neo-capitalism of the second half of the twentieth century.

There is another fact, too, which helps to explain the inadequacies of social theory at the present time. The rapidity of social change during the past century has confounded the thinker's effort to grasp the principal forces which are at work in modern societies. It is possible, for example, that the importance of classes and class conflicts in determining the course of social life has diminished in recent times, even though many of the issues which they posed remain just as significant as they were for Marx and the early socialists. However that may be, it is plain that other social groups and other divisions in society have been acquiring a new importance. The bonds of nationality, of language, of ethnic origin, of religious community, have been more strongly affirmed in many societies and have given rise to new social movements. The division between rich and poor nations is firmly established, and some radical thinkers have seen in the "third world" a new international proletariat, revolutionary in a way that the industrial working class in western societies has failed, or ceased, to be, and capable of achieving socialism. The conflict between generations has become more intense, and many of the protest movements in all countries express the resentments and aspirations of a younger generation much more than those of a class.

These considerations may be summed up by saying that two kinds of difficulty stand in the way of a *critical* social theory at present. One is that of providing an account of the development of modern societies which is genuinely explanatory; the other, that of connecting such an account with the aims of the socialist movement. It was Marx's great achievement to draw together in a comprehensive sociological theory of modern capitalism the major intellectual discoveries of his age in philosophy and social science; and to formulate a social doctrine in which, as I have argued elsewhere, the empirical confirmation of his theory could provide at the same time "a degree of rational and factual support for [his] moral convictions."[2] Marx accomplished what many other social thinkers, then and later—the Utilitarians, the Saint-Simonians, the Fabian socialists, the pragmatists—also attempted. But in the light of more recent social history his success may be questioned. The science of society and the social doctrine appear to be at odds: on one side, the socialist ideal; on the other, the intractable facts of changes in class relations and class outlooks. The rejection of ideology, by the American New

[2] "Karl Marx: Sociologist or Marxist?" *Science and Society*, XXX (1) Winter 1966, p. 23.

Left in particular, is not so much a spurning in principle of all ideology; that is, of any social doctrine which tries to set forth in some plausible relationship both an explanation of social events and a moral vision of a good society. It is a dismissal of those creeds inherited from the 1930s which now seem to fit very loosely to the facts of social life; and an expression of misgiving about what can now take their place.

These perplexities are experienced more acutely in North America than in Europe, and the rejection of ideology has been more extreme, leading in some circumstances to what recent critics have termed "mindless activism"—a new left-wing variety of American anti-intellectualism. The reasons for these differences are to be found in the history of social thought and social movements which I have briefly traced. In Canada there has not been an intellectual class able to develop a social theory based upon the experience of Canadian society. It is only now growing up, more obviously in French Canada than in English Canada; and its future depends upon the progress of the social sciences, upon the institution of a dialogue between French and English thinkers, and upon an association with active and broadly based movements of social reform.

The United States, a society much more numerous, wealthier, and longer established, should clearly possess much greater intellectual resources. Thus it is possible to trace, as I have done, the growth and decay of schools of critical thought which have some resemblance to those of Europe. Yet the resemblance is imperfect. Social criticism in the United States has been, until very lately, a somewhat weakly growth, both in stature and in influence. The social thinkers whose ideas have formed our modern consciousness have almost all been Europeans. They were the principal source of ideas for American thinkers, and only in one important case, that of the pragmatists, can it be said that a distinctive body of social thought was created which followed a partly independent course of development. Even then its intellectual and social influence was limited by the absence of any powerful social movement which might have responded to it, and by the general indifference to all intellectual endeavor.

Today the critic, in his role as expert, has a respected place in American society. As an ideologist—that is, as the producer of general ideas which criticize fundamental aspects of the social structure and culture, he may still be regarded with some suspicion or aversion. But even here here has been a change. Perhaps the very excesses of McCarthyism have produced a reaction. At all events the works of the radical critics are now read by a large public; and these critics have undertaken inquiries into their society more ambitious and thorough than have been attempted in most other countries in recent years. Aside from the major works of criticism which I discussed in earlier chapters, the studies which have been made of the social movements themselves, and a journal such as *Trans-action,* published since 1963, represent some of the most successful attempts in any country to direct critical social thought upon current issues. The new liveliness of social criticism in the United States owes much to the development of the protest movements, and much also to the importance of America's role in world affairs. In a society of such wealth and power, capable of doing such immense good or harm to the whole world, the social critic can scarcely fail to acquire a sense of the seriousness and urgency of his task. This is, perhaps, for the United States something like a Victorian age in which the actions and responsibilities of a great world power provoke a major undertaking of self-criticism. Only the assurance of the Victorian critics is still lacking, and the question remains whether radicalism can find some lasting embodiment in American society, or whether it will again be dissipated in one of those repeated movements of despair and withdrawal. At the turn of the century, the first editor of *The Nation,* E. L. Godkin, wrote: "Our present political condition is repulsive to me. I came here with high and fond ideals about America, for I was brought up in the Mill-Grote school of radicals. They are now all shattered, and I have apparently to look elsewhere to keep even moderate hopes about the human race alive." Hope revived during the progressive era, but it was destroyed by the war, and in the 1920s radicals once more said farewell to reform. Again there was a revival of radicalism in the 1930s, followed by a more shattering defeat in the 1950s; whereupon the end of ideology was proclaimed and a self-styled revolutionist could write: "I now think no one has a duty to interest himself in politics except a politician."[3] Will the experience of the 1960s be different? The answer depends upon whether the new radicalism can find some basis in society less ephemeral than a student movement, less confined than the Negro revolt; whether it can produce an ideology responsive to the doubts and complexities of our age and yet capable of directing action, with some hope of success, to plausible ends.

[3] Dwight Macdonald, *Memoirs of a Revolutionist,* p. 4.

SELECTED

BIBLIOGRAPHY

I. *General Works*

Egbert, Donald Drew and Stow Persons, *Socialism and American Life* (2 vols. Princeton, Princeton University Press, 1952). An essential reference work. The second volume contains a comprehensive annotated bibliography.

Hofstadter, Richard, *Social Darwinism in American Thought* (Revised edition, Boston, Beacon Press, 1955)

———, *Anti-Intellectualism in American Life* (New York, Alfred A. Knopf, 1964)

———, *The Age of Reform: From Bryan to F.D.R.* (New York, Vintage Books, 1955)

Lasch, Christopher, *The New Radicalism in America, 1889–1963: The Intellectual as a Social Type* (New York, Alfred A. Knopf, 1965)
Presents radical thought mainly by discussing individuals, some of them relatively little known. Conveys well the atmosphere of particular intellectual circles.

Parrington, Vernon L., *Main Currents in American Thought* (3 vols. New York, Harcourt, Brace, 1927–30). See especially Vol. II, Book II, Part III "The Transcendental Mind," and Vol. III, Book I, Part I, Chapter IV. Volume III was unfinished at the time of Parrington's death and is fragmentary.

Preston, William. Jr., *Aliens and Dissenters: Federal Suppression of Radicals, 1903–1933* (Cambridge, Mass., Harvard University Press, 1963)

There are anthologies compiled from some of the important liberal and radical journals:

    Christman, H.M. (editor) *One Hundred Years of the Nation: A Centennial Anthology* (New York, Macmillan, 1965)

    Luce, Robert B. (editor) *The Faces of Five Decades: Selections From Fifty Years of the New Republic, 1914–1964* (New York, Simon and Schuster, 1965)

O'Neill, William (editor) *Echoes of Revolt: The Masses 1911–1917* (New York, Quadrangle Books, 1967).

    Phillips, William and Philip Rahv, *The Partisan Review of Anthology* (New York, Holt, Rinehart and Winston, 1962)

See my comments on some of these anthologies in the text, p. 44 above.

II. *The Progressive Era*

Two influential books which heralded the progressive era are:

Bellamy, Edward, *Looking Backward, 2000–1887* (1887; new edition, New York, The Modern Library, 1951)

Lloyd, Henry Demarest, *Wealth Against Commonwealth* (1894; new edition, Englewood Cliffs, Prentice-Hall, 1963)

Bourne, Randolph, *Youth and Life* (Boston, Houghton Mifflin, 1913).

———, *Untimely Papers* (New York, The Viking Press, 1919)

On Bourne's place as a radical intellectual, see the study by Christopher Lasch, cited in the previous section.

Chamberlain, John, *Farewell to Reform: The Rise, Life and Decay of the Progressive Mind in America* (New York, The John Day Company, 1932)

A disillusioned account of the struggles of reformers against the trusts and political corruption.

Croly, Herbert, *The Promise of American Life* (New York, Macmillan, 1909)

One of the best statements of the political ideals which guided the progressive movement, by the first editor of *The New Republic*.

Dorfman, Joseph, *Thorstein Veblen and his America* (New York, Viking Press, 1934)

A well-known study of Veblen's ideas and of the character of American society in his time. See also a later study of Veblen: David Riesman, *Thorstein Veblen: A Critical Interpretation* (New York, Scribner's, 1953)

Sinclair, Upton, *The Jungle* (New York, Doubleday, Page and Co., 1906)

The most sensational work produced by the muckrakers.

Steffens, Lincoln, *The Autobiography of Lincoln Steffens* (New York, Harcourt, Brace, 1931)

Weinberg, Arthur and Lila (editors) *The Muckrakers* (New York, Simon and Schuster, 1961)
A good selection from the writings of the muckrakers, with notes and commentary.

Weyl, Walter, *The New Democracy: An Essay on Certain Political and Economic Tendencies in the United States* (1912; new edition, New York, Harper and Row, 1964)

————, *Tired Radicals and Other Papers* (New York, B. W. Huebsh, 1921)
The first of these books, by another editor of *The New Republic,* sets out a progressive political theory; the second examines the decline of radicalism.

White, Morton, *Social Thought in America: The Revolt Against Formalism* (new edition, Boston, Beacon Press, 1957)
An excellent study of the progressive thinkers, which examines the major writings of Holmes, Dewey, Beard, Robinson and Veblen.

III. *The Nineteen-Thirties*

Arnold, Thurman W., *The Folklore of Capitalism* (New Haven, Yale University Press, 1937)

Berle, Adolf, Jr. and Gardiner Means, *The Modern Corporation and Private Property* (New York, Macmillan, 1934)

Kazin, Alfred, *Starting Out in the Thirties* (Boston, Little, Brown, 1966)
Melancholy recollections of the intellectual climate of the 1930s.

Lynd, Robert and Helen, *Middletown in Transition* (New York, Harcourt, Brace, 1937).

Schlesinger, Arthur M. Jr., *The Age of Roosevelt: The Crisis of the Old Order,* 1919–1933 (Boston, Houghton Mifflin, 1957)
See especially chapters III and IV on the approaching crisis and the social and intellectual movements of opposition.

Simon, Rita James (editor) *As We Saw the Thirties* (Urbana, University of Illinois Press, 1967)
Includes essays by Earl Browder, Hal Draper, Granville Hicks, A. J. Muste, and Norman Thomas.

Wilson, Edmund, *The American Earthquake: A Documentary of the Twenties and Thirties* (New York, Doubleday and Co., 1958)
Parts II and III contain essays on events of the 1930s mainly reprinted from *The New Republic.*
See also the discussions of radicalism in the 1930s in some of the general works listed in Section I of the bibliography.

IV. *The New Radicalism*

Bell, Daniel (editor) *The Radical Right* (2nd expanded edition, New York, Doubleday, 1963)

Fromm, Erich, *The Sane Society* (New York, Rinehart, 1955)

Goodman, Paul, *Growing Up Absurd* (New York, Random House, 1960)
Examines the difficulties of the young generation in the USA.
Harrington, Michael, *The Other America* (New York, Macmillan, 1963)
One of the best accounts of poverty in the USA.
Howe, Irving, *Steady Work* (New York, Harcourt, Brace, 1966)
A representative of the "Old Left" argues with the "New Left".
Jacobs, Paul and Saul Landau (editors) *The New Radicals: A Report With Documents* (New York, Random House, 1966)
A good selection of critical writings with an introductory survey of the social movements.
Mills, C. Wright, *The Power Elite* (New York, Oxford University Press, 1956)
Newfield, Jack, *A Prophetic Minority* (New York, New American Library, 1966)
Presents the views and attitudes of the young generation of radicals.
Riesman, David, *The Lonely Crowd: A Study of the Changing American Character* (New Haven, Yale University Press, 1950)
────── *Individualism Reconsidered* (Glencoe, The Free Press, 1954)
Roszak, Theodore (editor) *The Dissenting Academy* (New York, Pantheon Books, 1968)
See especially the essay by Noam Chomsky, "The Responsibility of Intellectuals."

V. *The Social Movements*

Miller, Michael V. and Susan Gilmore (editors) *Revolution at Berkeley* (New York, Dell Publishing Co., 1965)
See also the essay by Sheldon S. Wolin and John H. Schaar, "Berkeley and the University Revolution," *New York Review of Books*, VIII (2), February 9, 1967, which examines the decline of the student movement.
Westin, Alan F. (editor) *Freedom Now! The Civil Rights Struggle in America* (New York, Basic Books, 1964)
A good selection from studies of the civil rights movement and from statements by participants. An earlier study of the Negroes which has become a classic is Gunnar Myrdal, *An American Dilemma: The Negro Problem and Modern Democracy* (1944; new edition, New York, Harper and Row, 1962, with a new preface by the author and a brief survey of the changes over twenty years by A. M. Rose).

VI. *Recent Social Criticism and Social Movements in Canada*

D'Allemagne, André, *Le colonialisme au Québec* (Montreal, Les Éditions R-B, 1966)
Julien, Claude, *Le Canada: dernière chance de l'Europe* (Paris, Grasset, 1965)
Knowles, Stanley, *The New Party* (Toronto, McClelland and Stewart, 1961)

On the history of the Cooperative Commonwealth Federation and the formation of the New Democratic Party.

Lipset, S. M., *Agrarian Socialism* (Berkeley, University of California Press, 1950)

Macpherson, C. B., *Democracy in Alberta: Social Credit and the Party System* (2nd edn. Toronto, University of Toronto Press, 1962)

Oliver, Michael (editor) *Social Purpose for Canada* (Toronto, University of Toronto Press, 1961)

Porter, John, *The Vertical Mosaic: An Analysis of Social Class and Power in Canada* (Toronto, University of Toronto Press, 1965)

Rioux, Marcel and Yves Martin (editors) *French-Canadian Society*, Vol. I. (Toronto, McClelland and Stewart, 1964)

INDEX